POUR

THE SELF-EMPTYING TRUTH ABOUT FULFILLING
YOUR PURPOSE

MERRICK DEANS

DEANS LIST ENTERPRISES, LLC

I dedicate this book to my God – the One who created me on purpose, with purpose, and for purpose. Thank You for the inspiration, insight, and endurance to accomplish what I never could on my own. This work, along with all of my efforts, is done unto You – for Your use and Your glory!

Amen.

CONNECT WITH THE AUTHOR
Merrick Deans

f facebook.com/merrickgdeans

y twitter.com/merrickdeans

O instagram.com/merrickdeans

CONTENTS

LOVE LETTER

Merrick,

When you first introduced the concept of *Pour* to me, I was honestly quite intrigued. Not because it was something new or something I had never heard of, but because it was different. It was deep and it was enlightening. Your theory of *Pour* opened up my heart and mind and I was personally rethinking my life and the way that I operated. I began to search within myself and wonder not just about what I was doing with my life, but about what my motivation was behind what I was doing – or why I was doing what I was doing. Was I really giving my all in my purpose? Did I trust God and others to pour back into me as I was giving? Was I holding on to things that needed to be given and shared with others? Just so many questions!

So, as great as this concept that you introduced to me is, you also gave me a new life assignment (more adulting!) to work on. The better part of me is grateful you expanded my thinking while the other part of me is now challenged to truly live my purpose in the manner it should be lived out.

Over the course of 8 years, we've had countless conversations that have sparked my interest or helped me to see life through a new set of eyes. That is what drew us to one another – our ability to share and converse in a way that I never grew tired of. Admittedly, some conversations have either been forgotten due to my lack of readiness to receive what you were saying or my lack of attention.

But *Pour...Pour* is different. It touched my heart and my ears differently than anything we have discussed.

Not only has your theory of *Pour* been expressed verbally and now documented (so proud of you), but I have seen you live out your words.

I can say without hesitation or exaggeration that you *Pour* every single day. In your business endeavors, your calling in ministry and your love and commitment to your family – you – **POUR**. And because you *Pour*, God is able to give you more. You have the capacity of handling it. You are an amazing steward over your life and what you have been blessed with.

I have told you for years how you leave me in awe over the dedication and discipline you have in your life. For someone like me that tends to struggle through that, you are truly an inspiration. I may not always express it, especially in my challenging moments, but that is what my heart feels for you. It is what my heart knows. And it is one of the main reasons why I love you so.

You made writing this letter so easy and seamless. I did not have to pull something from the sky or make up anything. You exemplify *Pour*. You live out *Pour*. You, Merrick Deans, *Pour*.

So, thank you. Thank you for sharing your life and light with us all. Thank you for sharing your heart and your mind with us.

We need this. The world needs this. It is time for us all to go beyond what makes us comfortable and feel good. It is time for us to take action and live our lives in the way God has called us to live them.

I am ready to *Pour*. And it is my hope and prayer that, after reading this, your readers are ready to do the same.

I love you honey-honey. Always share your light and heart with us all – even if we are not ready to receive or comprehend just yet. We will come around, I promise.

Your Forever Fan in Every Way,
Tiffany Deans

PART I

PURPOSE-FULL

And Jesus answered him, "Blessed are you..! For flesh and blood has not revealed this to you, but my Father in heaven.
  - Matthew 16:17 NRSV

REVELATION

We all have defining moments in our lives; points where some-thing happens that shifts the way we view and interpret ourselves, those in our immediate circles, and the larger world in which we live. Oprah Winfrey endearingly refers to these shifting points as "Aha Moments" and Doc Brown from the *Back to the Future* movie series would say, with great enthusiasm, "Great Scott!" when he experienced one of them. I simply call them "revelations". Though I have had quite a few revelations throughout the course of my life, there are two major ones that stand out from the rest. The collective result of my experiences during these two moments of discovery both clarified and solidified my reason for being gifted with life!

If I had to label each revelation, I would say that the first was "life-altering", in that it completely changed the value I had previously placed on my purpose; the second was "life-defining" because it truly solidified what my purpose was. I would like to think that my "life-altering" revelation, which happened at the decorated altar of the church I was married in, while my wife and I exchanged our vows, would have been the moment when the haziness of my life came fully into focus and my purpose was undoubtedly defined, but it wasn't. I mean, shouldn't one who is pledging their life to another be really clear about what value their life has and be keen on what their life was intended to accomplish?

In hindsight, because I wasn't fully aware of my reason for being born, I could only write my vows based on my capabilities rather than my calling. You see, it's one thing to say to the person you love "I will do this and that because I believe I'm able to," verses saying to them "I will do this and that because I was born to do it. Being with you is part of the reason I was put on earth!" Though it wasn't all-encompassing, the powerful revelation I had while standing in front of my bride, promising her the very best of myself, altered the way I looked at my life. I no longer wanted to commit myself to people or things without truly knowing why I was created and what I was created to do. It was in this moment that my values shifted and my purpose became the benchmark for my being; it would be the thing I would use to measure my plans, pursuits, and productivity against.

Yes, that was the moment my purpose became a priority, however, in order to complete it, I had to first find out what it was. It's funny how learning something new will often uncover how much more you don't know. This "life-altering" revelation quickly took me from obscurity to clarity and right back to obscurity, now realizing just how uncertain and unsettled I was about my purpose.

Fast forward two years and two months, I am next to my bride once again, only now I am at her bedside holding her hand and combing my fingers through her beautiful curly hair as she is preparing to deliver our first child. We have loved ones in the room and there are doctors and nurses cycling in and out, yet the only people I was focused on were my wife and my soon to be born baby girl.

> *Side Note: Let me pause for a second and say that life has a way, at times, of completely grabbing your full attention and forcing you to stop indulging in your personal wants, in order to focus on people/things outside of yourself!*

Witnessing the volume and intensity of the contractions on the monitor, feeling the movement of the baby preparing to exit the womb, and hearing the groans from my wife restricted my ability to be concerned with meeting any needs of my own. Bearing the physical and emotional heaviness of the needs of my girls in this moment produced another first for me. For the first time ever, I felt that my need was to have their needs met. I had crossed a fulfillment barrier that made it impossible for me to feel personally "fulfilled" or satisfied unless the needs of those I was responsible for and accountable to were met. This was the "life-defining" revelation that would come to define my purpose and ultimately my life!

Again, it would seem that this revelation should have come on my wedding day or even over the course of my two years of marriage prior to my daughter being born. In hindsight, I realized that it couldn't have come during those times because my personal needs, not my wife's, were my primary focus. I stood at the altar fully aware that my wife didn't "need" me, and frankly, I didn't "need" her either. We had managed to get through 30 years of life apart from each other as single independent adults, so what did we really "need" from one another? In my eyes, our wedding represented our choice to be together, not our co-dependence on one another. Don't get me wrong, I cared about my wife's needs but I didn't have an inherent belief that meeting them was part of my purpose. I thought that the best thing I could do for her and for our marriage was to make sure I was the best "me" possible; that meant fulfilling my own desires and meeting my own needs and not making it her duty or burden to do either.

Yet, when that beautiful baby girl came screaming into the world, I instantly knew that her and her mother were directly connected to my purpose. This was a clarifying revelation for me because, unlike my wedding day, I was well aware that my daughter could not meet her own needs. It was no surprise how easy it was for me to see that my daughter couldn't be her own father and that I was created to fill that role in her life. However, what did catch me off guard was the more difficult but very necessary aspect of this revelation; that just like my daughter couldn't be her own dad, my wife could not be her own husband!

She may not have needed me to help her to survive in this world, but she did need me to provide her with the things intended for her husband to give her; things like deep intimacy, loving counsel, a protective covering, and the coveted dual-income, lol. Things that she could not provide for herself. Likewise, having me as her husband enabled her to fulfill the distinct portion of her life and purpose that was intended to be a wife. We may not have been co-dependent on one another, but our purposes were. If a portion of my purpose was to be Tiffany's husband, then I would be unable to become all that God created me to be without her as my wife and that was a truth I could no longer deny nor take for granted!

Why did seeing the need of my family help to clarify my purpose? The reality is, it wasn't their need for me that clarified my purpose, rather it was the very nature of purpose that made its obscurity transparent to me. In the time since that moment of revelation, I started a journey to understand purpose. I didn't believe that it was just happenstance that I gained a sense of clarity about my reason for living in the moment when I was thinking least of myself. I didn't think it was just a coincidence that I felt most alive when I was seeking to meet the needs of others before and above my own. It was along this journey that I discovered that the nature of purpose, the true essence of its makeup, is *release*.

Nothing - no human nor animal - formed outside of human

hands has been nor can be created with the intent to extract from the world. Even if we choose to make personal gain our ultimate goal, we can only accomplish it by releasing something that is already within us. If your gain is to come through people giving to you, you first have to release something that provides value to them (e.g. product, counsel, labor, etc.). If your gain is to come through taking from others, you first have to release something detrimental to them (e.g., fear, deceit, domination, etc.). The common denominator is that none of us are born empty. We are all born full of something the world needs!

As beings who are full: full of perspective and insight, full of ability, full of energy, and full of transformational qualities, we were all put here to release what's inside us, out to the world; we were made to pour! Therefore, the closer we get to the concerning needs of others, the closer we get to our purpose. The closer we get to meeting those needs, the ones we were intentionally shaped and created to meet, the closer we get to fulfilling that purpose.

Now, being overtly aware of the nature and reality of purpose, it has become my burden and my blessing to consistently and liberally pour into needs that are not my own. Yes, it started with my family, but I have sought out other areas in my life where I am led to pour, for I know those are the people and places directly connected to my purpose. If I chose to center my abilities, time and energy on fulfilling my personal desires, I have no doubt that my life would be impressive. However, I've come to understand that by choosing to center my resources on releasing, to fulfill my purpose, my life doesn't simply impress others - it impacts them!

I pray that impact becomes the desire and objective for your life as well, and that this book will ignite a number of your own revelations, which bring about clarity and understanding for your journey. I encourage you to keep your mind open to challenging concepts and remain malleable to change because that is the hard but necessary path of progress. In execution of my purpose, I have shared what has been revealed to me and it's my hope that it will move you closer to a life focused on purpose and positioned to pour...God bless!

Chapter 1

A GREATER END

I wrote this book to serve as a catalyst for self-discovery. Therefore, I figured I'd start it at the place where all discovery begins - on the other side of a question mark.

What is your purpose?

No, the question isn't groundbreaking but it is practical. In fact, I'd be willing to bet that most people, including you, have posed this question to themselves in one form or another. Perhaps it was "What's my why?", or "Why was I created?", or maybe "What was I born to do?" Regardless of how the question is framed, based on a generally accepted philosophical under-standing, answering it is the first step to attaining a richly fulfilled, successful, and truly meaningful life.

I mean that's really why we ask the question to begin with, right? It's because we hope there is more out in the world for us than just the monotonous and, at times, seemingly meaningless jobs, classes, errands, activities, and responsibilities that unintentionally, yet very noticeably, consume our schedules. Though we press through each day managing what's currently on our plates, in the back of our minds, many of us loosely hold on to the belief that we weren't born to simply exist in the world, but that we were put here for a real reason and that life has much more to offer us than what we've been settling for. But what exactly do you think life has to offer you? What is it that you are looking to gain from this "purpose-filled" life you so eagerly desire?

Maybe it's comfort and control that you expect to receive; a life where you call the shots and work when, where, and how you want to, not having to always bend to the will of others. Perhaps it's influence and impact that you desire from this life; being able to shape outcomes and change people and things for the better. It could be possessions and positions you aspire to obtain; having a life that affords you access to everything your heart desires. Whatever your "purposeful" life looks like, the reality is that many of us yearn to find and complete our purpose because we believe it's the gateway to that very life. In other words, **we aren't trying to fulfill our purpose; we are trying to use our purpose to fulfill ourselves** (i.e. to provide, produce, and promote our personal desires).

"True happiness... is not attained through self-gratification, but through fidelity to a worthy purpose." - Helen Keller

These words, shared by Helen Keller get to the core of the *purpose problem*, which is that self-gratification/self-interest/self-centeredness stands in conflict to a worthy purpose, when it comes to attaining "true happiness", or fulfillment. In an effort to solve this problem, allow me to present a new construct to you regarding your purpose and its relation to your life. One that takes *personal fulfillment* off the self-indulgent pedestal most of us have placed it on, no longer making it your ultimate goal in life, and replaces it with a much greater end – an end that leads to *purpose-fulfillment* instead. In this new structure, you'll no longer view your purpose as the means to getting the life you want; rather, you'll use the life you have as the means to success-fully complete, or fulfill the purpose you've been given.

THE ATTRIBUTES

Now, if I'm going to have any success at getting you to fully adopt my proposed concept of purpose-fulfillment over personal fulfillment, I must first help you to comprehend it by re-contex-tualizing two key attributes typically associated with purpose, which are *meaning* and *resource*.

Meaning

It's likely that you have looked to your purpose to give your life substantial meaning, believing that when you finally accom-plish your purpose (i.e. your purpose-driven goals) then your life will become significant and be worth something of value to you and to others. The truth is, this is an unfruitful approach to attain-ing, or should I say, realizing your life's meaning.

The allure of meaningfulness is that, in a mirage-type fashion, it appears to be the missing component for those of us who are eager to find ourselves and who strongly desire to leave our indelible mark on the world. Since we can't just pick up meaningful lives at the store, we get stuck in uncertainty and confusion and the freeing question then becomes, "how do I get a life that has meaning?" This is where many of us falsely insert purpose! We mistakenly think that if we identify and complete the thing we were born to do then it will all click; we will be overwhelmed with a strong sense of clarity about who we are and our worth will be undeniably established. Because when you accomplish something that matters, then you matter, right? *Wrong*!

You can discover a sense of purpose and execute all the amazing things you believe that purpose requires of you, yet still feel insignificant and meaningless. Please know that what you do is not always synonymous with who you are; good people are capable of doing bad things and bad people are capable of doing good things. In the same train of thought, accomplishing meaningful objectives doesn't make your life meaningful. You can do things that matter and still feel as though your life doesn't.

To rely on the completion of purpose as the determining factor of your life's significance, though unfruitful, is natural and very understandable, especially given the structure of our modern, media-influenced "show-and-tell" society. As a result of people posting and praising their accomplishments and the accomplishments of those they idolize, day in and day out, we have developed a societal complex that says, "I only matter when I achieve". In fact, it's actually worse than that, we're realistically at the point now where we believe that "I only matter when I achieve what few others haven't or can't". We have adopted a mindset that causes us to compare ourselves to our contemporaries and calculate our value based on our ability to separate ourselves from the pack by climbing higher and going further than the next person. Therefore, unless we make more money, have more attendees, take more trips, sell more products, work more hours, have more anniversaries, and so forth, then we are "less than" and thus are insignificant to ourselves and to the world we aim to impact.

The problem is not that we look to our purpose for our life's meaning; the problem is <u>how</u> we look to our purpose to validate that meaning. We should look to our purpose as an indicator that we matter; attributing our life's meaning to the fact that we have a purpose and were created for a reason. Instead of adopting this view, we try to attribute our life's meaning to the achievement or completion of that purpose. In other words, we attach little to no significance to the value of having life, only to what we accomplish with it! This skewed reality exists in opposition to how God intended for us to view our purpose and approach life as He (this is not to suggest God has a gender) originally created it.

Here, let me explain. In the Bible, there are two different accounts of the creation of mankind (i.e. male and female). Both help us to understand the intentionality of God and his reason for creating humans. There are a number of differences that exist between the first and second narratives; differences in the way things were created, differences in when they were created and even where they were created. Despite these differences, what they do have in common is their identification of a need prior to the creation of humans. Genesis 1:26-27 details the first account then Genesis 2:4b-7 highlights the second account:

First Account: *"God said, 'Let us make humankind in our image, according to our likeness; <u>and let them have dominion</u> over the fish of the sea, and over the birds of the air, and over the cattle, and over all the wild animals of the earth, and over every creeping thing that creeps upon the earth.' <u>So God created humankind</u> in his image, in the image of God he created them; male and female he created them."*[1]

Second Account: *"In the day that the Lord God made the earth and the heavens, when no plant of the field was yet in the earth and no herb of the field had yet sprung up — for the Lord God had not caused it to rain upon the earth, <u>and there was no one to till the ground</u>; but a stream would rise from the earth, and water the whole face of the ground — <u>then the Lord God formed man from the dust of the ground</u>, and breathed into his nostrils the breath of life; and the man became a living being."*[2]

Now, in the first account, God had a dominion problem. He had created every living thing that inhabited the earth and needed someone(s) to oversee or have dominion over all the animals and insects. In the second account, God had a tilling problem. He hadn't enabled the earth to produce plants or herbs for two reasons; because he had not yet caused it to rain and because there was no person to till or work the ground. He fixed the water issue by allowing a stream to rise, but he was still in need of a tiller. Both of these realities thrust the creative hand of God to give life to humankind. Therefore, it's not a coincidence that in the verses immediately following each of these passages identifying a need in the earth, God purposefully brings humankind into existence in order to meet it.

So, what does all this have to do with the validation of your life's meaning? I'm glad you asked! The point is that your life's meaning comes from having purpose, not from completing it. In our new construct of purpose, **your life had *meaning* from the moment you were conceived because it was intentionally created to meet an identified need**! Much in the same way that a car has significance and value before it fulfills its purpose. You pay thousands of dollars to purchase a car before it has taken you back and forth to your destinations, transported any of your belongings, or blasted your favorite music while in traffic. It's because the car's value is based on what it was created to do, not what it has already done; likewise, your life's significance or meaning is derived from having purpose, not completing it.

To drive this nail in a little further, let's go back to the biblical example. Adam and Eve never had to accomplish the requirements of their purpose in order to justify their existence or prove their worth. They were supposed to have dominion over all the animals, yet they allowed the serpent to direct their actions. Adam was supposed to till and care for the Garden of Eden, yet he defiled the land by eating from the forbidden tree and was later kicked out. Eve was supposed to be Adam's helpmate, yet she conspired with him to disobey their Creator. If the significance of their lives had been based on their execution of purpose, Adam and Eve would be worthless. Fortunately for them and for us, when intentionality proceeds your existence, the creation of your life is the determining factor of your meaning-fulness to the world. Put another way, that which is given purpose is significant; in fact, it is because your life is significant that you have the ability to fulfill its purpose, not the other way around!

The last thing I will impress upon you regarding the attribute of *meaning* is on a much more personal note, but one that will hopefully help to clarify how your life's significance is an attribute of life creation, not purpose completion. I'm not sure if you have ever had to endure the loss of a child prior to delivery, whether through miscarriage, abortion, or stillborn, but it's a lingering pain that I wouldn't, in anger or in jest, wish on anyone. Unfortunately, my wife and I know from experience the width of the hole that this type of loss can leave in the heart of a family and it is because of our familiarity that we send love and prayers to those who have endured this reality.

> **Reflection:** It was on my first Father's Day, less than a year after experiencing the joy of having our baby girl, Ava, when my wife and I found out that we were unintentionally going to have our second child. I would like to say that my initial reaction was one of happiness, but it was actually one of questioning and confusion; asking God questions that I already knew the answer to, like "How did this happen?" and "Is this for real?" It wasn't by immaculate conception, so I knew exactly how it happened and my wife's symptoms along with the symbols on the pregnancy tests confirmed that it was

definitely for real. All that said, it wasn't confusion I was feeling, it was actually fear!

I was gripped with fear in what should have been a celebratory moment because my wife and I, only months prior, tripled our mortgage by purchasing a new house. To throw another log on the fire, in an effort to avoid debt, we also dipped into our savings to furnish this new house. Now, to add kerosene, we were also paying an obscene amount of money for daycare in our new neighborhood while shelling out hundreds for diapers, formula, clothes and supplies for our 8-month-old daughter. Outside of the money, the intimacy in our marriage was waning at best; deep meaningful communication was morphing from a privilege into a chore, romance was a luxury, and sex had become a rare commodity due to health challenges, fatigue from adulting, and the mounting emotional and physical pressures caused by ailing parents. In fact, the first time we had been intimate in a very long time was weeks before the pregnancy tests read positive. So, after seeing the results of the test, all I could think about was how the financial, physical, and emotional balance we were desperately trying to begin to get back in order was now, once again, crumbling before me.

After Tiffany and I dropped a few tears and gave it to God, we jumped into preparation mode to try and ready ourselves for the baby, whose arrival was seemingly fast approaching. It was right then and there that our family life began to shift in a major way; we started cutting down on expenses and bolstering our savings back up; we started executing things we had been putting off since Ava's arrival. Tiffany and I talked more and spent more quality time together than we had in months; we knew uncertainty lied ahead so we prayed without ceasing, looking for comfort and answers wherever we could find them!

After nine weeks of shifting, it was time to finally see what it was all for, it was time to see our little bean-shaped baby on the monitor and hear their heartbeat for the first time. This being our second go 'round, we knew what to look and listen for - I will never forget seeing my daughter's tiny heart fluttering on the screen while hearing her strong heartbeat, before any of her body parts had even started to form - so I waited with much angst and anticipation to hear our second baby's heartbeat knowing that this is what would make it real for me!

One of the top things I aim to develop, in this life, is patience because I barely have any and the few drops I do have were quickly evaporating while the technician made multiple attempts to get the size measurements and slowly hand-peck the data into the system. Wishing we had the technician from our first pregnancy, I started to think to myself that this lady must be new because she was taking forever to get to the part where we hear the heartbeat; yet despite this, I stayed quiet, held my wife's hand and waited. After the tech unexpectedly went to get the doctor, I soon found out that the delay wasn't due to her proficiency but rather to God's plan. Teetering between accepting reality and holding on to hope, we made one last plea to God to reverse the results before heading into the doctor's office to discuss our "options". Leaving the exam room, the weight of knowing I would never hear the sound I was anxiously waiting to hear laid on my chest; it appeared that reality had won and we had to accept that the embryo on the screen, rather the embryo in my wife, was present but lifeless.

Over the next three to four months, following that dreaded appointment, Tiffany and I worked through our loss and focused on continuing the momentum that we had started when preparing for the baby. We developed a new outlook on our lives, both individually and as a couple, and a new value on time, which became evident in our daily activities and decisions. Both of us pursued career and ministry opportunities that our previous desire to "play it safe" caused us to initially undervalue or overlook. The hard but gratifying truth about losing a piece of the family circle is that it forces the remaining pieces to draw closer together to help close the gap. Whether it was to cry, laugh, or converse, Tiff and I grew closer to our daughter, to one another, and to God.

Looking back over the time preparing for and healing from our incomplete pregnancy, I couldn't help but think of the huge shift that manifested in our family as a result of this baby. Having never breathed their first breath, never uttered a sound, nor having ever taken one step, this unborn angel changed the direction of our household and pushed their mother and I closer to our ultimate destiny, which we now understand was their purpose. So, it is with great conviction that I hold fast to the belief that each and every one of us are conceived with a purpose and that purpose is the hook from which our life's significance hangs. Our unborn baby's life, having never accomplished anything of significance on earth, had tremendous meaning, and the good news is, so does yours!

Resource

The second key attribute tied to purpose is *resource* – by resource, I mean anything of value that can be used to achieve or obtain something else. In a simple job model, your work produces a paycheck, which is your resource for doing and getting other things. As it relates to purpose, it's generally believed that executing your purpose produces an abundance of resources in your life. You may hear people, who claim they're operating in their purpose, refer to having more energy, money, time, insight, passion, and a bunch of other great things; they claim these resources are made available to them as a result of executing their purpose. Those feelings may be genuine, however, the identified resources are not the product of executing purpose, quite the opposite, they are the provision for executing purpose. In our new construct, **your provision of tangible and intangible resources is given to you by your Creator (i.e. your Source) to aid you in completing your purpose**. As I mentioned in the introduction, you are born full! So, the fruits of purpose are not what you gain from fulfilling it, but rather what you have to pour into the needs of others.

Martin Luther King, Jr. provides a great example of the provision of resources FOR purpose, not FROM purpose. A list of Dr. King's capabilities would no doubt be long and perhaps even controversial, depending on who you ask, but one key capability that can be agreed to by most is his gift of sight. I don't mean "sight" in the physical sense, though I never saw a picture with him wearing eyeglasses; I mean sight in the metaphysical sense (i.e. hindsight, foresight, insight, and oversight).

He often conveyed his sense of sight in his speeches by describing to us a world that had not yet manifested. He vocally painted images of the promised land he saw when, by faith, he declared that "I have been to the Mountaintop!" He again used cinematographic language to project his prophetic *Dream* to millions of people. His resource of sight was not the result of him having already executed his purpose of bringing a divided nation together; it did not come to him as a gift or reward for completing all he was born to do, but rather it was provided to him so that he would be able to fulfill his purpose. His ability to communicate, draw supporters, and evoke compassion and commitment were all resources that enabled him to carry out his God-given purpose. In the same way, all the resources that you currently have and will have at your disposal are not the fruits of your labor, they are the seeds needed for your labor to produce God's intended outcomes in the people and places he created you to impact.

The Truth

My intent for redefining these attributes is to shift your mindset and help you to both assess and understand your purpose in a newly enlightened way. This new mindset is fully aware that we were not born to be filled but rather to be emptied, and at its core lies the truth about purpose; that it was given to you, but it's not for you. As Helen Keller conveyed, it's not for your convenience, it's not for your comfort, nor is it for your compensation; it is exclusively in service to and for the benefit of your counterparts and contemporaries. Your ability to fulfill your life's purpose hinges upon your ability to grasp the distinct elements of this truth.

Element 1: The fact that your purpose was given to you by your Creator means that you cannot decide what it is for yourself! The created thing can never dictate the reason it was created; only the creator of that thing can decide and articulate the intended functionality and operation for what they've created. Simply put, you cannot pick your purpose, you can only discover and fulfill it.

Element 2: The fact that your purpose is not for you means that it was given to you for people and things outside of yourself. Things that you do which are meant for your benefit and pleasure are important, but they're not related to the fulfillment of your purpose; they are your hobbies! Purpose requires an output of resources that serves the needs of the people and the environments that God intended for you to change for the better. Going back to the creation narratives, humankind's purpose was to serve their surroundings (i.e. animals, earth, plants, etc.), not themselves.

These elements of truth, related to the fulfillment of your purpose, are woven into the descriptions of the previous attributes. Specifically, your life's *meaning* is not based on the value of your accomplishments but rather on the value of your assignment; additionally, your *resources* are not gained from your efforts, but given for your purpose. Once again, it's not about you – it's not about what you've achieved nor what you've acquired – it's about those you've been created to benefit and what you've been given to do it with. Accepting the revelation of these attributes will enable you to approach fulfilling your purpose with the right mindset, expecting only to carry out your Creator's intentions on earth rather than trying to use purpose solely for your benefit.

Understanding the self-denying truth required to fulfill your purpose is critical, however, it is pointless unless you're able to effectively apply it to your life. Put in the form of a question, this sentiment would be stated as such, *"How do I execute what I was created to do in a way that fulfills my purpose rather than my personal desires?"*

Before we explore the answer to this question, let me add this disclaimer about your purpose not being about you.

Disclaimer: Even though your purpose is not intended to fulfill you, know that it is still worth pursuing! Fulfilling purpose requires you to pour out to others what has been placed within you and it is the pouring that creates the necessary space in your life to be poured back into. You have already been filled! You've been filled with capabilities, creativity, characteristics and so forth. Therefore, it is a trivial pursuit to try and fill something that is already full. When you focus your efforts on pouring, then you will stop trying to be FULFILLED and instead seek to be REFILLED.

Those who aim to be refilled understand that they were once filled and, just like a car pulling up to a gas station, they return to their Source to be filled again and again. Being refilled requires that you know the One who filled you in the first place and to constantly seek Him to replenish you with all the resources (e.g. strength, patience, love, ideas, peace, etc.) you need to continue to pour out. Fulfilling is a self-pursuit, but refilling is a source-pursuit, which requires self-denial. Be careful not to confuse self-denial, in the fulfillment of purpose, with self-neglect. Self-denial is acknowledging your personal needs/wants, along with your inability to adequately meet them yourself, and choosing to entrust their satisfaction to God as you pursue your purpose. Conversely, self-neglect is choosing not to acknowledge your personal needs/wants at all. I am not advocating for you to ignore your personal needs, rather I am encouraging you to stop trying to be the one who meets them.

Streams cannot provide their own water; they need rivers, rivers need oceans, and oceans need rain. Likewise, you are not self-sufficient either, you cannot look to fill yourself through the execution of your own purpose. Your purpose can't be pulled from, it can only be poured into, and you can only be filled from an outside Source! The good news is, God has created other people and given each of them a purpose that is intended to help meet your needs, just like yours was given to meet theirs. If you allow others to complete their purpose in your life, trust that you will be fulfilled; you just won't be the one doing it!

Chapter 2

MORE THAN WORK

Generally, when you think about executing your purpose, you only think about completing the work related to it. For example, if you believe your purpose is to cook and I ask you to execute your purpose, you will most likely start prepping ingredients, grabbing cookware, and proceed to throw down in the kitchen. Though that's relatable, for our understanding, the execution of purpose must be expanded beyond just doing the work of your purpose. **To fully execute your purpose, you must not only do the work, but you must do it for the right reason and do it the right way.** Doing it for "the right reason" is nothing more than completing the predetermined, or intended, objective of your purpose. Similarly, executing your purpose "in the right way" simply means to do it how it was intended to be done.

To best explain this concept, let's stick with the example of cooking being your purpose. If you were to cook food all day every day, do you believe that your existence on earth would be justified, your destiny realized, and your purpose fully executed? I would venture to say *"No"*!

I'm quick to say no because purpose is not free-floating! Webster defines *Purpose* as "something set up as an object or end to be attained..."[1], so, by its very definition, purpose has an objective attached to it. There was an assignment that needed to be completed in the world and you were created for the purpose of completing it. In other words, you were made to not just do, but to do in order to achieve a specific outcome.

Like with any assignment, just doing the work alone does not complete it; your work needs to be deliberate and directed to successfully finish the job. Just doing the work alone is similar to a plumber just plumbing in your house, working on your bathroom toilet when you intended for them to fix the kitchen sink, or a mechanic just working on your car, replacing your engine when you needed your axle fixed; or in-line with our initial example, a chef just cooking in the kitchen, making a rack of lamb and steaks for a vegetarian dinner. You weren't put on earth to "just do" anything! Done without intention, the work, the activities, the tasks, and the action items you execute will make you busy, but not impactful, and certainly not purposeful!

To fulfill all that your purpose requires of you, or meet its objective, you must be keenly aware of its three components: **WHY, HOW, and WHAT**. Comprehending these components in a practical way is necessary in order to successfully execute your life's purpose. It's important because not knowing the reason why you were made to cook or understanding how your cooking is supposed to impact the world will cause you to miss the intended mark.

Not only that, but it's far more likely that just cooking alone will result in you experiencing the highs and lows of happiness and frustration with no lasting sense of impact or progression from your efforts. The reason for this is not because you misidentified your purpose or that you aren't working to your full capacity. It's because you're only doing what you are purposed to do, "the work", with no awareness or understanding of why or how you should be doing it. Complete execution of purpose requires that you know WHY it was given to you, HOW to effectively carry it out, and WHAT it is before and during your execution of the work related to it.

The Golden Circle

The Why, How, and What components are not readily applied to fulfilling purpose, however, the concept of using these questions to focus the motives and execution of efforts is not a new one. The Golden Circle is a theory expounded upon by author and speaker, Simon Sinek, which he details in a number of his Ted Talks and in his book, *Start With Why*.

The premise of his theory is that, in order for individuals and organizations to effectively gain supporters or customers, they must first identify and communicate their reason for **why** they do what they do. Second, they need to explain **how** they do it, and third share **what** it is they do or have to offer. This was an intentional redirection from the common approach of individuals/organizations first, and most prominently, detailing their offerings (i.e. what they do), then trying to differentiate themselves by highlighting how they do it better than their competition, and finally, with little significance, sharing why they do it. Sinek determined that the Why should be the differentiating factor between individuals/organizations and should be the guiding light for their How and their What.

He bases the effectiveness of this order of thought and communication on the biological structure of the human brain. One section of the brain is the Neocortex, which controls our rational, analytical thought and language; another is the Limbic Brain, which determines our feelings, behavior, and decision making. When individuals/organizations attempt to appeal to the Neocortex first, by leading with What they offer, then even if they provide a great deal of convincing information, it still may not evoke a favorable decision (e.g. a sale, a vote, or membership) because they have not effectively engaged the part of the brain that controls behavior. Thus, the person being solicited doesn't feel the offering is for them even if all the information tells them it's a good service or product. On the other hand, when an individual/organization leads with Why and then follows with How, before detailing the What, it appeals to the Limbic Brain first and evokes emotion and, ultimately, a favorable decision from those who agree with and potentially even share the individual's/organization's Why, or purpose. This type of decision just feels right to the person in a way they can't communicate; even if it doesn't make total analytical sense, it's what their gut tells them to do.

Sinek's theory has been used to improve the outreach efforts and marketing campaigns of many organizations by helping them to internally identify and externally communicate their purpose before and above their process or products. Understanding the method's intended use, I believe with the right reengineering, it can be expanded to serve our needs as well. If our aim is to execute purpose in a way that makes purpose-fulfillment the ultimate goal (not self-fulfillment), then we can focus our mindset and efforts by applying the Golden Circle principles to purpose-fulfillment and redefining its components in the following way:

1. **The *"Why"*** - This is the will of your purpose (*Objective*)
2. **The *"How"*** - This is the way of your purpose (*Operation*)
3. **The *"What"*** - This is the work of your purpose (*Outlets*)

In my estimation, the majority of people approach the mystery of purpose in the wrong manner. Much like in Sinek's observation, when left to their own wherewithal and devices, they first try to figure out the *What*. Once they think they've found what it is they were born to do, which few people feel they actually do, they start doing the work of their purpose in the way and at the capacity that is feasible for them. In other words, they ambitiously determine the *How* based on their available means (e.g. capital, network, opportunities, etc.) and personal ability. After grinding it out the best way they "know how" (pun intended), they begin to use personal and societal measures of success to analyze the outcome(s) of their efforts, in hopes of uncovering an ultimate reason, a deeper meaning, or – referencing our new terminology – a *Why* for their work. Here's an example of this approach:

> **"What-First" Example:** *Jane likes to bake and all of her family and friends love her culinary creations, so much so that Jane believes baking is **What** she was born to do! Since baking is Jane's purpose, she spends a lot of time trying to figure out **How** she can get as many of her treats to others as possible. She sells some on her website and at bake sales as part of her side business, and makes free baskets for hospital patients during the holidays. Although it is very time-consuming, expensive, and tiring, Jane loves it when people enjoy her baked goods, it makes her feel needed and accomplished in the world, and that is **Why** she wants to continue to bake for as many people as she can!*

Those who pursue purpose in a *"What*-First" manner, like Jane, make the *What* the target instead of the arrow; they focus their efforts on executing purpose-driven tasks rather than focusing their purpose-driven tasks on meeting the objective, or *Why*, of their purpose. But if they are fixated on the work of their purpose, how do they know if they are actually fulfilling their purpose or not? *They don't!* The only thing they can conclude is how they either feel about doing the work or feel about the results of the work; personal fulfillment is their only factor for determining whether or not they are executing their purpose. Therefore, if the work is meaningful and makes them feel good, like Jane, then they think it's their purpose. However, if the work is meaningless and makes them feel bad, then they think it's not. Because feelings are fleeting at best, this approach causes the person to be in constant search of their purpose; the moment the work is unfulfilling or the results undesirable, they start seeking out another *What* in hopes of recapturing the lost feelings of fulfillment and significance again.

This approach to purpose is flawed in a couple of ways. The first is that their objective is not to fulfill purpose, but rather to fulfill self. The second is that the person's primary focus is on the *What* and not the *Why*. I previously addressed the detriment of the first flaw and the importance of making purpose a selfless pursuit. Regarding the second flaw, when the *What* takes precedence over the *How* and *Why,* then you will only exist in the world; you will only do what you are able to and not what you were born to! For those of you currently pursuing purpose in a "*What*-First" way, allow me to offer a better approach. In order to realize the true power of fully executing your purpose, you have to put the cart back behind the horse. To be specific, you have to reverse the order of your purpose pursuit and start with the *Why*.

Why

Following the Golden Circle method, the *Why* of your purpose is primary to the *How* and the *What,* so the first step to executing your purpose is to uncover its objective or the reason it was given to you to begin with. You have to ask yourself "why was I given a purpose?" or "what was my purpose intended to actualize in the world?" Though I want you to ponder the question, for the sake of progression, let me just tell you the answer. The reason you were given a purpose is to **Fill**! You were created and shaped to fill a specific and pre-existent void between God and others, which further drives home the point that your purpose is not for your personal fulfillment. Take a second and imagine your purpose as a puzzle piece. On the left side of the puzzle piece is a portion that is open, and on the right, is a portion that extends.

Both sides of your puzzle piece are intended to connect it to other pieces, but each side connects in a different way. The left side, where the opening is, is the receiving side; it can only connect to the adjacent piece by accepting the portion that the other piece extends to it. In opposing fashion, the right side is the giving side; it connects to its adjacent piece by extending its portion to connect to that piece's receiving side.

The *Why* of your purpose works through the design of this puzzle piece, in that its objective is to be a functioning gap-filler between the two disconnected pieces on both of its sides. The piece on the left side of your purpose is the provision of your Creator, who desires to meet the needs of the people, which are represented by the piece on the right side of your purpose. Though the people on the right are in need of all that God has for them, they aren't appropriately shaped - they don't have the right ear, heart, capacity, capability, etc. to receive everything they need directly from the Source. **This is why your purpose was given to you...to** *fill* **the void between divine provision and earthly need!**

Disclaimer: To be clear, God intentionally shapes us to fill certain gaps in order to meet specific needs, which has two very critical implications. The first is that you are not created to fill every gap nor meet all of the needs of the people that your purpose connects you to, only the need(s) you have been resourced and positioned to alleviate. To drive this point home, in keeping with the illustration, notice that the giving portion of the Purpose piece doesn't connect to all of the receiving portions of the Needs piece, it only connects to the one portion that it fits.

The second implication is that you are not the only one that has been created to fill gaps and meet needs. God has created every single one of us to fill a gap between Him and others! That said, you have to know that you too need other people to fulfill their purpose in your life, just like they need you to fulfill yours! For the needs you are designed to meet, you are the piece in the middle (receiving from God directly), and for the needs you possess, you're the piece on the right (receiving from God through the fulfilled purpose of others).

Once I began to truly understand the *Why* component of my purpose, I soon realized that **I wasn't born to just DO something in the world; I was intentionally created to BE something in the world.** Many people mistakenly try to identify their purpose by searching for work to perform. They ask themselves questions like "what was I created to do?"; trying to decide whether they were made to cook, or sing, or farm, or write, or design. They should instead be searching for the space they were made to fill, pondering questions like "who, where, and what was I created to be?" I don't mean "be" in the sense of putting a title to the work, like being a singer or a farmer. I mean "be" in the sense of existing! Existing in a space that is void of provision.

Every need that is realized in the earth is the result of something missing that should be present. Referencing the biblical creation narratives I previously shared, God didn't have a need for humankind when the world was empty and without form; the need arose, and human creation sprang forth, once the things He had created before humankind (i.e. land, sea, animals, etc.) were lacking something that they were supposed to have. What we can see in this story is that there is a difference between undefined space resulting from emptiness and defined space resulting from a gap. Emptiness exists when something is not present. On the other hand, a gap exists when something is not present between two or more things that should be connected. God's need for us in the earth arises out of gaps, not emptiness; that means your purpose is not meant to just do something in undefined space, it's intended to fill a defined space to establish or restore the connection between the disparate things (i.e. Him and His people).

The true needs of people, not their glorified wants, result from gaps in provision between us and God. These gaps are not created from a lack of provision from God, but rather from a lack of access to God's provision on behalf of His people. Now, a need can be pacified without the gap that created it being filled; yet without filling the gap, the need will continue to regenerate. The only way a need can be fully met is if the gap that's causing it is filled. This is the difference between pacifying a man's need for food by giving him a fish and satisfying his need for food by teaching him to fish; the former only addressed the regenerative need while the latter addressed the gap. Therefore, in order to truly satisfy the immeasurable and unending needs of His children, God has created access to His provision by tailoring a purpose for each of us that requires us to BE in the gaps between Him and others, not to simply DO tasks and activities in empty space.

The reason you have to lead with *Why* is because it's the litmus test for your purpose. Regardless of how the thing(s) you do makes you feel or what you gain from it, if its objective is not to fill a gap between Provider and People, then it's not connected to your purpose. The *Why* doesn't just tell you what to look for when pursuing purpose, it also tells you where to look. Those who take a "What-First" approach, like Jane, search for purpose in their work by trying to uncover meaning and personal fulfillment from their efforts. On the other hand, those who adopt a "Why-First" approach instead, search for ways to put their purpose to work! They are clear that the objective of their purpose is defined by who, where, and what they are and thus it permeates into every facet of their life. Every relationship, every role, every responsibility has the potential to expose a gap that their purpose was intended to fill.

Having this expanded sense of purpose helped me to approach life with a more encompassing mindset; I stopped trying to live a double life of pursuing purpose apart from who I was. Essentially, I had two proverbial hats that I would continuously put on and take off depending on what I was doing. I had a "Purpose Hat" that I put on when I searched for and executed meaningful work in an attempt to fulfill my purpose, and I also had a "Merrick Hat" that I put on when I was away from my work, filling roles that correlated to who I was, like being a father, husband, friend, etc. This dynamic of putting purpose down to be "myself" and picking it back up to be "meaningful" makes sense if your understanding of purpose is confined to what you do in the world. **However, if it is stretched to encapsulate who you are in the world then purpose can't be put down and picked up throughout the day, it can only be completely ignored or fully lived out**.

When I was wearing two hats, I struggled with the concept and practice of maintaining a "work-life" balance; I initially felt as though my time with my family was constraining me from successfully completing my purpose and vice versa. However, as I evolved from a Doer to a Gap-Filler, I started to see that the needs of those close to me, specifically those of my wife and daughter, weren't obstacles for me to work around as I pursued my purpose. On the contrary, they were ordained openings that my purpose was designed to fill. It became clear that God made provision to meet every single one of my girls' needs and part of the reason He created me was to facilitate that transfer in certain areas of their lives. This is not to say that they aren't able to receive straight from God – they both have individual purposes that allow them to transfer from Him to others, including myself – but it is to say that some of the things He has for them, they aren't shaped or positioned to directly receive. There are physical, emotional, mental, and spiritual manifestations that God intends to produce in both my wife's and daughter's lives, which are dependent on me filling the gaps my purpose was customized to fill!

Hopefully, this insight has started to get your brain churning a bit and thinking about the various areas of your life in a new way. What you once saw as a potential distraction from, or in competition with, your purpose should now start to look like another area where your purpose can be executed. The *Why* of your purpose is not to fill self but to fill a definitive gap between God and His creation, which you have been uniquely shaped to fit. Getting back to our puzzle example, the receiving side of your purpose is intentionally shaped to connect to God in a way that allows Him to provide you with the *resources* needed to fulfill your purpose. In the same way, your giving side has also been intentionally shaped for you to connect with those you are meant to pour your *resources* into in order to meet specific needs. It's for this reason, knowing that your purpose has been intentionally shaped to *Fill* is vital to you completing it!

Before we move on, let me first clarify that not everyone is appropriately shaped to connect to your purpose. Therefore, **you must be mindful not to try to alter the giving portion of your**

"puzzle piece" purpose to force an unintended connection with everyone! Many people, including myself, have fallen into this trap, generally in one of two ways; either they try to connect their purpose to *unintended people* or they try to connect their purpose to intended people in *unintended ways*.

> **Unintended People:** You connect to unintended people when you seek out empty spaces that you can benefit from by utilizing your resources; this either leads to or results from self-fulfillment, not purpose-fulfillment, being the dominant goal for your life.

> **Unintended Ways:** You connect in unintended ways when you attempt to either meet wants instead of needs or meet needs you weren't created to meet. This can happen when you try to be someone's "everything" by attempting to fill all their gaps and/or give them everything they want.

For me, it was the former (Unintended People), I intentionally sought out people (i.e. individuals and organizations) that would allow me the opportunity to personally benefit from using my resources. I am a Management Consultant by trade, in essence, I help companies and the Federal government to develop and implement strategies and solutions to improve their organization and its operations. My God-given ability to find connections between seemingly disconnected things and to articulate undefined and complex concepts afforded me a number of opportunities and job offers throughout my career. Over the years, I worked my way up to the point where I was able to pick and choose who I connected, or worked, with and what I worked for. In theory, I would change the giving portion of my puzzle piece to fit whatever need that would benefit me the most; whether it was for more money, more flexibility, or more autonomy, I was seeking connections to fulfill my desires, not my purpose. To be clear, I'm not beating myself up for trying to excel in my career; it's okay to make connections to get what you want out of life. On the contrary, I'm being critical of my inability to ALSO connect with those I was created to connect with, in any substantial capacity, in order to fulfill my purpose. In fact, I had gotten to the point where I thought I was fulfilling my purpose by making connections based on my personal intentions rather than my Creator's. Looking back, I missed out on so many opportunities to share my resources with people that I should have helped, simply because I was overwhelmed with helping myself.

> **Side Note:** *You cannot properly identify the people you were created to connect with by looking through the lens of personal benefit. Your skills and abilities will enable you to make a difference in the life of the person(s) or organization, but you will not be able to complete your purpose. Connecting with the wrong people will either cause you frustration because <u>they don't have the capacity</u> to receive all that you have to give, or it will cause you fatigue because <u>you don't have the capacity</u> to give all that they must receive to meet the need.*

From my experience, I can say that starting with the *Why* is the only way you can truly fulfill your purpose. Understanding the *Why* will allow you to broaden the scope of your purpose and accurately identify the gaps you were created to fill in completion of it. It's only when you know your intended gaps that you can connect to the right people in the right ways. Even still, as important as it is to make the right connections, you also have to be keen on how to transfer your resources to those in need. Yes, you are made to fill gaps, but how do you go about doing it, what are the means to meeting that objective? The *Why* of your purpose is primary, but it isn't exclusive, the *How* and *What* are just as critical.

How & What

So, now you know that the true objective, or *Why*, of your purpose is to *FILL* specific gaps between heaven's provision and humanity's need! The profundity of that statement is not in its wording, but rather in the depth of its reality. Understanding and accepting this reality is the key to fully comprehending the *How* of your purpose and being able to fulfill it in a selfless way. If I were to liken the *Why* of your purpose to a door frame, representative of its stable unchanging nature, and liken the *What* of your purpose to the door, which moves when and in the direction needed by those entering and exiting (I'll explain this a little later), then the *How* would operate as the hinge between the two. If the *How* is correctly identified and effectively implemented in your life, it will enable you to maintain your purpose's one steady objective (door frame) while at the same time allowing you to do the multitude of things required to execute it (door swing). It's for this reason that I've made the *How* the very focal point of this book! But before I deep dive into the *How,* let me quickly shed some light on the *What* of your purpose.

As we previously covered, the *What* is just one of three components of your purpose so you can easily deduce that it is not the totality of your purpose in and of itself. Even though there is a *Why* and a *How* to your purpose, the majority of people hang their hats solely on the *What* because it is the tangible expression of the reason they were created. Not to mention, it is also much easier to comprehend internally and convey to others externally. I mean, if someone asked you what your purpose is and you started telling them about divinely filling conceptual gaps to meet earthly needs and door hinges, it may not go over so well!

That said, it's a slippery slope to limit your purpose to the *What* because the only job of your *What* is to carry out the actions needed to meet the objective, or the *Why*, of your purpose. To try and reduce your complete purpose to just the *What* is inadequate in and of itself, yet many people often take it a step further and try to limit the *What* of their purpose to just one thing. It's likely that you are at this point now, trying to define your purpose by one activity; if it is, then you need to **STOP!** Attempting to squeeze your great purpose into one role, one place, one service offering, or one activity does nothing more than minimize the possible actions you can take to complete your God-given objective and ultimately fulfill your purpose!

My dad, being from Queens, used to say, "son, there is more

than one way to get to New York," alluding to the multitude of entry points into the city whenever he was trying to encourage me to find another way to get to my desired outcome. His sentiment applies to your *What* as well, there is more than one way to execute your purpose!

There is a one-to-many relationship between the *Why* and *What* of your purpose, meaning you can do many different things to meet your one objective. T.D. Jakes provides us an example of this concept. Being a man who wears many hats, he preaches, hosts conferences, writes books, produces films, makes TV and radio appearances, and a number of other things. When asked why he operates in so many different capacities, he noted that his purpose is to communicate and he fulfills his purpose through his work in each of these mediums. To contextualize his thoughts into our construct, what he was saying is that his *Why*, like yours and mine, is to fill a gap between God's intended provision and the needs of people utilizing his resource of communicating powerful messages. That said, he was able to find multiple *Whats*, or outlets, with which to share his resource and ultimately complete the objective of his purpose. I say this to say that you shouldn't allow the *What* of your purpose to be boxed into one medium or intermediary. The challenge and the goal of your purpose is to remain faithful to your *Why*, remain aware of your developing resources, and remain open to the many *Whats* that may present themselves as avenues for you to pour from. Remember, just like there are many routes into New York City, **there is more than one way to execute your purpose!**

Okay, so now that I have given my two cents on the *What*, let me step off my soapbox and get back to the *How* of your purpose. When you start to think about the *How,* you have to think about operations; it's asking yourself the very piercing but necessary question, "how does my purpose operate?" Is your purpose executed in a way that makes you the benefactor or the beneficiary? Does it make non-refundable deposits into others' accounts or make investments in them, expecting an increased personal return? It's important to know because the way in which you operate, or carry out, your purpose makes all the difference between you just working at it and you actually fulfilling it.

Being a Management Consultant requires that you have a good understanding of Operations. Regardless of the project, Operations is the most impacted and impactful area when it comes to change because it is the lynchpin between the inputs and outputs of any organization or system. Whether it's turning capital into profits, raw materials into merchandise, or code into software, your ability to get from start to finish is dependent on the effectiveness and viability of your operation. The same is true when it comes to fulfilling your purpose; your ability to have the objective of the *Why* be completed by the work of the *What* is based on the effectiveness and viability of the operation of the *How.*

Allow me to take this analogy a bit further to help make my point. When I am working on a project that requires me to identify and solve an organizational problem, the first place I usually assess is the organization's processes (i.e. its Operations) that are directly and/or indirectly contributing to the undesired result(s). However, before I start identifying and documenting the steps and stakeholders in the process, I meet with my client to find out the intended result or objective of the process. I have to gain this information first because the process should be directly aligned to the objective, meaning it should have been designed to yield the result(s) intended by the client. The objective establishes the benchmark for which to measure the results of the process against and identify the gaps between what the process should be doing and what it actually is doing. Herein lies the criticality of operations, when purpose is not being effectively executed, the issues rarely, if ever, lie in the objective (the *Why*) or the actions taken to meet the objective (the *What*). The issues are usually found in how the actions are being executed (the *How*). Simply put, **it's not the *Why* or the *What*, it's the inadequacies of your *How* that is keeping you from fulfilling your purpose**!

Knowing the criticality of your purpose's *How* is key, but it is only half of the equation, the other half is understanding what the *How* is. To help you contemplate this, ask yourself what ways have you tried to identify and execute your purpose. If you are like most people, you've taken time to think about your passions and talents; the things that you're good at and enjoy doing. You try to identify ways to monetize your gifts and/or figure out how you can get as many people as possible to buy into you. More than likely, you try to find ways to do what you love in order to get what you want out of life, believing that your fulfillment is the objective of your purpose.

Well, now that you know the true objective of your purpose is to fill gaps in order to meet the needs of others, what does that reveal about the way you are intended to complete it? How can you meet the needs of others when you are looking for ways to meet your own needs? The reality is, *you can't*! The only way you can complete the objective of your purpose, the only way you can fill that gap, is by pouring out to others the resources that have been placed within you. If you want your purpose to function in a way that doesn't just make your work interesting, but impactful, you can't pull from others; you have to **POUR** into them!

Let's quickly recap the Golden Circle method in our context. The *Why* of your purpose is to fill the gaps between God's provision and humanity's needs; the *How* is to fill those gaps by pouring your resources into those you were made to connect with; and finally, the *What* is to do whatever work you are equipped and capable of doing, to pour what has been placed within you. Revisiting our previous "*What*-First" example of Jane and her baked goods, let's now see what it looks like when she chooses to start with her *Why* instead of her *What*.

> **"Why-First" Example:** *Jane aims to positively impact the lives of others because she believes that's **Why** she was put on earth. She gladly shares her gifts and talents to benefit those she can, which is **How** Jane is able to make a difference in her community and abroad. Of all the things Jane does, baking is **What** she is most recognized for; everyone enjoys her baked goods, so much so that Jane thought it would be a good way to pour love and encouragement into others. Each of her delicious treats, including those she sells and those she donates, come wrapped in beautiful packaging with a positive message, which makes all the difference for all who partake!*

Reconfigured in a "*Why*-First" way, we can see how Jane not only rightly aligns her operation and outlet(s) to her objective, but she also is more likely to stay committed to fulfilling her *Why* even if her *What(s)* changes over time. Perhaps she will lose her passion for baking or choose to explore other interests. Either way, she will still be able to fulfill her purpose in whatever she does because it is not tied to a *What*, but her one true *Why*. Like Jane, as long as you continue to pour out your resources in an effort to fulfill the needs of others entrusted to your purpose, then you will be able to produce the impact you were created to make in the world, no matter what you choose to do!

Improve Your View

Perhaps discovering that pouring out to others is how you fulfill your purpose wasn't an earth-shaking revelation, but my hope is that it was at least a perspective-shifting one! Perspective is everything in the game of purpose because the way you view the objective and operation of your purpose will determine how you assess and interpret the outcome of your efforts when pursuing it. If you see your purpose as a tool to attain a life that will be self-fulfilling and personally rewarding, then you will structure your operation to withdraw from those you aim to connect with. Also, you'll inherently evaluate your purpose based on the outcome of your work, using indicators that measure self-fulling things, such as your income, advancement, comfort, etc. Therefore, something will only be considered as part of your purpose if it makes you enough money or makes you happy enough to continue pursuing it. On the other hand, if your perspective of purpose is that it's an end and not a means; if you believe your purpose was given to you so that you can fill the gaps between God and others, through pouring, then you will structure your operation to deposit into those you connect with and your indicators will be much different. How you measure your execution of purpose will ultimately shift from evaluating *pull* indicators to *pour* indicators. They will go from the amount you gain to the amount you give, from your level of contentment to your level of completion, and from what you profit to what you produce.

How does your purpose operate...what is the means by which you carry out the tasks to execute it? Does your purpose facilitate you being poured into like a cup or does it operate as a spout for you to pour out to others, similar to a pitcher? Those who adopt a cup perspective of their purpose view its objective through the lens of their emptiness, in turn, structuring their purpose to withdraw from others to fill themselves. They aim to connect with people who can aid in filling their empty areas and materialize their personal desires. If they want more money, they find people who can provide additional income, if they want more exposure, they find people who will follow and promote them; if they want more access, they find people who have large networks and influence. I am not condemning this type of operation in general because, at its core, it is simply networking, marketing, and business/career building. I am, however, condemning it in specificity to the fulfillment of purpose because it is predicated on their emptiness rather than the emptiness, or need, of the people they were created to pour into.

If you desire to fulfill your purpose, you must view its

objective through the lens of your fullness rather than your emptiness! By doing so, your perspective will enable you to see the needs of those you were born to serve, without being obscured or obstructed by your own, as it relates to the completion of purpose. Furthermore, you will be able to structure your purpose to deposit by developing effective ways of finding the empty cups of others and impactful ways of pouring into them from your pitcher. Like Michelle Obama, Tony Robbins, Jay-Z, Ellen DeGeneres, Bill Gates, Oprah Winfrey and our initial example, T.D. Jakes, along with a host of other influencers, once you structure your purpose to pour, the outlets can become endless!

Personal feelings of inadequacy and emptiness, in relation to purpose, do not come from a lack of gain or achievement; they are the result of being full and having no place to pour! They come from your attempts to continuously gain and having no more capacity to hold what you're pursuing. Most of us operate in a constant state of being at full capacity but don't know it. We're oblivious to it because our perspective is focused on attaining the little we don't have rather than using, or pouring out, the much that we do have.

If you saw a person at the beach trying to collect seashells into a bucket packed to the brim with sand, you might think they were a bit strange. Now, if they got overly frustrated at their constant failed attempts to keep the shells in the bucket along with the sand, swearing that the bucket has room, you would think they were pure crazy. That is what we are doing when we operate at full capacity. We think that our capacity to be filled is based on what's not in our bucket (the shells) rather than what is (the sand). Just because you don't have all the things you want in your life doesn't mean you don't have something that is wanted, or better yet, needed by others. Your job is not to go out looking for more things to make you feel full. Your job is to go out and find someone who needs to build a sandcastle but has no sand...**you need to pour!**

Not only do you create room in your life to receive when you pour but the irony is your personal feelings of fulfillment are in direct correlation to your usefulness, not your acquisitions. Simply put, the fulfillment you seek happens when you empty what's in you, not when you gain what's missing. "Well-doing" is tied to your ability to get for yourself while on earth, but "well-being" is tied to your ability to give of yourself in fulfillment of your purpose. If you want to be full then focus on getting and doing more and more for yourself, but if you want to be fulfilled, or better stated, "refilled", then you must make room by pouring out your resources to others.

Your pour creates the necessary space internally to receive the new things God is trying to deposit within you, both directly from Him and through receiving the purposed pour from others. New ideas, new concepts, new creations, new skills, new gifts, new connections - new, new, new! Your Source has an unending abundance of resources He is able to refill you with and as you release to fill the gaps you're currently in, He will re-commission your purpose to fill greater, wider, deeper gaps.

If you are going to use your life to effectively impact the lives of the people and the world around you, you must continuously empty yourself of all that God has placed within you. In order to truly fulfill your purpose, you have to alter your operation to pour! To that end, it is my intent to journey with you throughout this book to transform your mindset, and ultimately, your method for executing your purpose, from pulling to pouring. In the spirit of practicing what I preach, I'm employing these pages to share with you the resources I've been given in an effort to fulfill my purpose and move closer to operating as a pitcher and not simply as a cup!

Chapter 3
FILTER YOUR FLOW

This is not intended to be a religious-minded or theologically polarizing book, however, many of its principles, which I'm sure you can tell by now, are rooted in biblical insights and spiritual revelations. That said, those familiar with the walk and ministry of Jesus Christ are likely aware that service was at the epicenter of all that he did during his time on earth. The *What* of Jesus' purpose doesn't call for much debate because it consists of the things he was most known for, which were teaching the lost and performing miracles. He used his resource of revelation to uncover God's will through parables (teachings) and uncover God's power through signs (miracles). The question of the *Why* and *How* of his purpose begs for a more complex response and, depending on who you ask, it often receives one. For simplicity's sake, I'll summarize the biblical evidence and say that the *Why* of Jesus' purpose was the same as mine and yours; it was to fill the gap between God and humanity so divine provision could meet the needs of the people. Restated, the objective of his purpose was to bring the Kingdom of Heaven to Earth and his *How* was by pouring out to others through service. Jesus makes his operation for fulfilling his purpose clear in Matthew 20:28a, saying to his disciples, *"the Son of Man came not to be served but to serve."*[1]

Service is not only germane to the purpose of Jesus Christ; it is germane to purpose period! What Christ was saying was that if I, in my divinity, was sent to serve, then know that you in your humanity were made to serve as well. Though this makes a compelling case for me, I understand not everyone subscribes to biblical teachings. The truth is, whether you follow Christ or not, one thing that is undeniable is that you can't fulfill purpose in isolation by only getting things from and doing things for yourself. Anything that is created to only serve itself is completely void of purpose because the condition of the world and the people who inhabit it would be the exact same had that thing never been created! Who would create a car with the intention of having it only drive itself where it wanted, when it wanted or a phone that only called whoever and whenever it chose to do so? Yes, it's important to know you are here for a reason but it's just as, if not more, important to know that the reason is to benefit others. You can and are encouraged to benefit yourself along the way, but know that it's for your pleasure, not for your purpose.

In order to fulfill purpose, you have to do something for one or more people outside of yourself; you have to impact your environment; you have to enrich the people, organizations, and places you are connected to! It's this reality that makes pouring relevant to the execution of purpose because pouring is the means by which you do things for others, it's your tool for affecting change, it's how you produce your intended impact in the world.

So, what does service have to do with pouring? Great question!

Pouring out to others is how you fulfill your purpose but there are a lot of things that reside within you that can find its way into your flow. It would be nice if we, as humans, were only comprised of good things like love, patience, kindness, peace, and so forth. However, the reality is, we're not. We're a collection of mixed emotions and experiences that are both good and bad. I believe the majority of us mean well but are inconsistent in maintaining those good intentions as we pour out our resources to the world. We all struggle with something(s) that causes our well-doing to be ill-received by those we aim to pour into; whether it's a lack of patience, time management, attention to detail, or concern, your issues will, at times, infiltrate your outputs. That said, **if we are going to truly meet the needs we were created to meet, we must purify our pour by filtering it through service!**

The effectiveness of service to function as the universal filter for everyone's flow, at first glance, may seem shallow in thought because of how society has traditionally watered down the term "service". We have appropriated the word in such a way that "service" has become much more synonymous with "offering" than "selflessness". For example, when companies list out all the things that they are capable of doing for their clients, they call them "services". Businesses advertise their brands by making statements such as "serving the community since 1940"; and those who perform maintenance refer to their work as service (e.g. servicing a car or a refrigerator). This generic use of the term has conditioned us to think that all endeavors, which provide a benefit, happen through service and that we are serving others by simply offering them something of value, but this is not so. Providing a service to others and serving others are two very different things that we must first clarify to really grasp the intended function of your filter.

Many may inaccurately assume that it is compensation that separates these two understandings of service; believing that when you provide a service to someone, you get paid for it, and when you serve someone, you don't get paid. You can genuinely serve others, in fulfillment of your purpose, and be compensated for it; there are many people who get paid really well for fulfilling their purpose. The real difference is in the *intent* of your service, not the outcome. When you provide a service to someone, you are offering a capability of value with the intent of generating personal gain, but when you serve someone, you are using your God-given resources to address an earthly need with the intent of alleviating it. With the former, you evaluate the potential return of meeting the need (i.e. compensation, exposure, access, etc.) to determine whether or not to pursue it and to find the most resource-efficient way(s) of doing so. With the latter, you simply evaluate the need to determine the best resource-exhausting way(s) (i.e. the *Whats*) to meet it.

Though the distinction of *intent* is primary, it is not all-encompassing. There is another line that separates service offerings from serving and that line is *sacrifice*. Now, sacrifice comes in different flavors and truthfully both of these types of service require a form of sacrifice, so I will delineate using a personal example.

I started a business that was not purpose-driven in the least bit. Sure, I had good intentions, but they were mostly derived from my personal desire for autonomy and more money. My business partner and I identified a number of skills and competencies we had developed as consultants and created a company focused on marketing and selling those resources for a profit, which again, there is nothing wrong with. We both had to sacrifice money, time, and a number of other things to get that business off the ground; it wasn't easy, but to us, it was worth it because we felt we had more to gain than to lose. This type of "pay the cost to be the boss" sacrifice is the prerequisite to personal gain and, to be honest, I quite admire it! Yet still, there is a difference between the type of sacrifice needed to gain and the type needed to serve.

Service-centered sacrifice is self-sacrifice, it requires you to intentionally give of yourself for the gain of others. It takes place through a process of self-emptying that happens when you pour out your resources to those you were born to serve. This type of sacrifice will still cost you money, time, and energy – it cost Jesus his life – but the difference is, it is intended to benefit others by meeting their need, not yours.

The way that you use service to filter your flow is by only pouring out to others resources that have passed through the two components of service: *intent* and *sacrifice*. Your resources must intend to alleviate the need of those you're connected to and must be given through self-sacrifice. This is important because it removes your feelings and flaws from the intended transaction between God and others. What if they don't pay you the agreed-upon amount or pay you on time? What if they constantly critique your work or ignore your suggestions? What if your spouse or your kids aren't doing what you want, when you want it? Are you going to allow your frustration, discontent, hurt, and anger to pollute your pour – to the point where you do for others but you do it with an attitude, or out of spite, or solely for compensation – or worse, stop pouring altogether? If you pour out of service to those your purpose has connected you to, then your feelings will be present but not primary because you have made the relief of others the intent and have sacrificed yourself (i.e. your will, your wants, and your way) to fulfill your purpose, your contentment will no longer be an inadvertent prerequisite for your pour.

Consider Your Concerns

When your pour shifts from a self-centered to a "service-centered" operation then you are able to fully optimize your impact! This might sound like a big transition - to go from focusing your pursuits on self-gain to focusing them on bene-fiting others – but it's not. In fact, it's natural for us to be more mindful of others than ourselves; the problem is, we are mindful of the wrong things!

We should be mindful of the needs of others that are concerning to us and how we can fulfill our purpose in their lives by helping to meet those needs. Instead, we've been conditioned to be mindful of what people think about us (approval), mindful of their shortcomings (hating/gossip), and even mindful of their successes (idolization). As a society, we are so fixated on others that billion-dollar industries have been developed simply by meeting the human desire to have access to other people's lives. Social media platforms, "tell-all" books, reality TV, and tabloids generate obscene amounts of income from massive public consumption due to misplaced mindfulness!

So, why can't we just mind our own business? The reason it's hard for us to put blinders on and only be concerned about what we have going on and nothing else is because that is not how we have been designed. You were not made to disengage from the world and operate in a self-indulging, self-fulfilling, self-consuming silo; you were made to connect with others in order to *Fill* gaps!

You were made to notice the needs of others and the ones that stand out to you the most, the ones you feel are most problematic, the ones that are the hardest to ignore and of the most concern to you, those are the ones you were created to alleviate! If you have trouble identifying the needs you were born to meet, start taking an inventory of your complaints. This is helpful because we often complain about the things we're subconsciously most concerned about. Your complaints are unique to your perspective and often reveal more about you than the thing(s) you're complaining about.

It's not coincidental that not everyone is bothered by and complains about the things that agitate you to your core; the lack of employee development at your job, or the unsafe facilities at your child's school, or the underserved demographics in your community are of concern to you for a reason! The reason is because your skills, experiences, abilities, and intelligence all inform you that better is possible. You may not know how to make it better and you may not be capable of doing it alone, but you have taken the first step to service because you've become aware of a concerning need, that negatively impacts others, which must be met!

Therefore, the transition that has to happen is not going from being selfish to selfless; the transition is going from engaging the people and things around you in the context of self (seeking to get what you want) to engaging them in the context of service (seeking to give what you have). The goal is to get you to stop centering your efforts on exclusively improving your life in comparison to others and to start centering your efforts on fulfilling your purpose in connection with others.

Make a Decision

To accomplish the goal of re-centering your approach to purpose, we must transform your mindset by continuing to shift your perspective. In other words, we have to alter the way you view your life, view yourself, and view your stuff in relation to the completion of your purpose. The best way to transform some- thing is to specifically and intentionally address each of its key components in order to minimize the bad and maximize the good. This method to produce change is relevant in any area of life. If you want to transform your relationship, address your communication techniques, time spent together, gift-giving, etc.; if you want to change your business, address your expenditures, sales, inventory, and so forth; and if you want to change your mindset, you have to effectively address your perspectives, assumptions, expectations, and anything else that causes you to engage the world in the way you do.

The first step to realizing a substantial and sustainable transition in your life is making a decision to do so! Before you can start addressing anything, you have to become aware of your need for change and then decide to make it. Some of you are able to make decisions very easily. By the end of the first chapter, you already determined that you needed to pursue your purpose differently and started thinking of ways to pour out your resources to meet the needs of others. Though I respect and commend your decisiveness, I can't stand it because of how unsure and doubtful you all make people like me appear!

Now, for all of my indecisive brothers and sisters, let me reassure you that there is nothing wrong with you, you are simply analytical and prefer all the available information prior to making a well thought out and, most of the time, overly-calculated decision! If you are still on the fence and are wrestling with whether or not you need to change the way you view and carry out your purpose on earth, I've provided a simple three-step process to help you weigh out and ultimately make this decision.

1. **Discover** - identify your current mindset by determining what you presently value (ask yourself *"what am I putting my effort toward?"*)
2. **Diagnose** - analyze the results that your current mindset is producing and determine the gap between your current outcome and your desired outcome (ask

yourself *"is my effort getting me where I need to be?"*)

3. **Decide** - choose whether to keep doing what you're doing or to make a change, then decide what that change will be (ask yourself *"do I need to do something different? If so, what is it?"*)

The first question will help to frame your current way of thinking by taking an inventory of your personal values. What we value often determines how we assess and interact with the world around us; we tend to work for and even fight for the things we value the most. If you value equality then you might sacrifice your freedom or even your life to attain it. If you value money then you might manipulate or even kill someone to get it. Regardless of the item or idea, your mindset is shaped by your values; your mindset operates as the middle man, turning your values into action by informing and directing your efforts. Therefore, if you want to know and eventually change what your mind is set on achieving in this world, then you have to identify and, if need be, change what you value.

Once you have identified the values that are feeding your mindset then you must determine if the outputs (i.e. actions, fruits, results, etc.) it's producing are what's intended for your life. As I mentioned before, purpose cannot be selected by the created, it can only be given/determined by the creator of that person or thing. So, your answer to the second question is not based on whether you are getting the results you desire, but whether you're getting the results your Creator intended; it's determining if your values are aligned to your purpose's *Why* or to your personal desires.

After you've inventoried and assessed your current supply of values and results, you should be adequately equipped to introspectively and honestly answer the third question. Your answer is critical to your transformation and will determine whether you need to keep reading or not. If you answered "no", then you are satisfied with the results you've been getting in your current understanding and pursuit of purpose. If you have not been required to pour into others through service, then your "no" means that you are okay with basing your success on achieving what you're capable of doing rather than what you've been created to do; that you are content with having a self-sustaining existence on earth, but not an impact in it. However, if you've acknowledged your need to change by answering "yes", then you have made the bold and necessary decision to progress beyond the purpose-less limits of self. I not only applaud your decision but I also encourage you to keep both this book and your mind open!

Throughout the remaining chapters, I will guide you in making the transformative shift from a pull-minded to a "pour-minded" pursuit of your purpose. I will help you to execute this shift in your current mindset by addressing the key components of your motivation for fulfillment. Each of the following chapters will explore the contrasting aspects of each component and enable you to attain true success by executing your purpose through service-filtered efforts instead of self-fulfilling ones. You were given a purpose, which is to provide God-supplied resources to resource-lacking people and there are many ways you can provide those resources to those who need them. The question is, by what means will you disseminate your resources? Will you use the resources you've been gifted to obtain the things that you want but don't have, or will you pour out your resources through service, to meet the concerning needs of others? Will you employ your resources to meet personal desires or purposeful needs? You can have a *purpose-full* life, but in order to do so you have to become *self-less*!

PART II

SELF-LESS

For you were called to freedom brothers and sisters; only do not use your freedom as an opportunity for self-indulgence, but through love become servants to one another.
   - Galatians 5:13 NRSV

MOTIVATION

As I grow in wisdom, which has come as a result of both intentional pursuit and experience, I have learned that behind every person's movement stands a guiding motive. So, as much as I desire for you to pour out to others all that has been placed within you, I know that my efforts to alter your actions are futile if I do not first attempt to change what motivates them. The 19th-century American minister and social reformer, Henry

Ward Beecher, described the moving force of one's motives in this way, "God made man to go by motives, and he will not go without them, any more than a boat without steam or a balloon without gas."

Though Beecher's references may be a little dated, the message is still very relevant because each of our actions as humans are tied to an intentional or unintentional motive. We eat because we're motivated by hunger, we sleep because we're motivated by fatigue, we speak because we're motivated by thought or feeling, and so on and so forth. It's for this reason that we have to examine and address our motives when seeking transformational changes in our lives.

I mentioned in Chapter 2 that the primary focus of this book would be on the *How* of your purpose because it operates as the lynchpin to you fulfilling it. It's to that end that Part II is dedicated to exploring your motives because your motives fuel the *How*, or the function of your purpose! Simply put, if you are motivated to fulfill yourself then you will pimp your purpose to get what you want from others, but if you are motivated to fulfill your purpose then you will pour out to give what you have to others. Therefore, my job is to guide you in exposing, examining, and evolving your motives to align them with the true objective of your purpose, which is to pour!

When we think about motivation, we tend to think about it one-dimensionally, but the reality is, there are two sides to motivation. Millions of people pay crazy amounts of money each year for motivational speakers to throw gas on their internal fires; they are focused on being encouraged to get to where they are going, to be motivated to go from mediocrity to domination.

However, the key to understanding what motivates you is not just looking at what you are motivated toward, but also assessing the source of your motivation. It's understanding both where your motivation comes from and where it is propelling you to!

If we were to only address your source and not the destination of your motivation then you would be doing the wrong things for the right reasons. Likewise, if we were to correct your destination but not your source then you would be doing the right things for the wrong reasons. My goal is for your intentions and actions to be aligned and aimed toward fulfilling your purpose, for the right reasons, doing the right things.

In an effort to meet my goal, we will dive into both the source and direction/destination of your current motivators, to transition them from pulling resources to pouring them into your purpose. Not only will we address both dimensions of your motivation, but I will also seek to alter how you monitor and assess the results of the actions you're being motivated to take. Because if you are doing the right things for the right reasons, but have no way of determining if you are maintaining it, then you will likely revert back to what fulfills you and not your purpose.

Part II Section Key

Chapters 4-6 are each structured to address the key aspects of your motivation (i.e., Source, Steps, and Signs) based on the following section outline:

Inclination - Natural human perspective and/or approach

Complication - Issues with the natural inclination(s)

Solution - Necessary corrections to address the identified issues

Application - Approach to implement the solution in a practical way

Chapter 4

FROM SELF TO SERVICE

SHIFT THE SOURCE OF YOUR MOTIVATION

T he first dimension of your motivation that we will address is its *source*. It's asking the simple question "what is motivating your actions?" This is foundational because it gets to the heart of why you pursue the things you do and ultimately take the actions you take. Though we are all different, there are some human inclinations that many, if not all, of us are naturally born with; as these inclinations mature over time, and through conforming experiences, they cause us to develop a mindset that is motivated by "self" rather than one motivated by "service".

To be clear, a mindset motivated by "self" is different from being "self-motivated"! Being self-motivated means that you don't need an outside force to push you to pursue the thing(s) you desire to attain. On the other hand, a mindset motivated by "self", or a "self-mindset" is rooted in logic and/or emotion that aims to meet personal needs before or in lieu of meeting the needs of others, in your pursuit of fulfillment or success. To clarify, the former is being self-starting, the latter is being self-serving.

Those who operate from a self-mindset inherently believe that fulfillment can only be attained when their personal needs are fully satisfied. Though this may be innate to your being, it is contradictory to the completion of your life's mission. In order to become the person God created you to be, you must overcome the propensity to put self-fulfillment before and above purpose-fulfillment. To achieve this, you have to consciously and intentionally shift your source of motivation from self to service. And in order to choose service, you have to first understand why self instinctually motivates your behavior as a human being.

Inclination

Most of us are pretty clear about the things we are motivated to do or attain; we know what we want. However, the freeing question is "why do we want what we want?" Unlocking the source of your natural motives will give you the necessary insight into your pursuits and behaviors, needed to effectively complete your purpose. Much work has been done to gain an understanding of human motives, most notable is that of American psychologist, Abraham Maslow [1]. In his 1943 paper, *A Theory of Human Motivation*, Maslow proposed that human beings have a hierarchy of needs that innately motivate our desires and behaviors. According to Maslow's theory, people generally have five main types, or levels, of needs: Physiologi-

cal, Safety, Belongingness & Love, Esteem, and Self-Actualization.

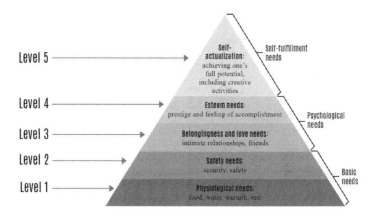

Not only did Maslow's theory identify the five levels of
needs, but it asserted that each level had to be relatively satisfied
before the individual would be motivated to satisfy the next level
of needs. For example, one would be solely motivated to first be
fed and hydrated before they could be motivated to find safety
and security. They would then need to feel safe and secure in
order to be motivated to establish loving relationships, and so on
and so forth up the hierarchy.

While Maslow's hierarchy of needs has been widely accepted
and respected in the psychology field, it has also been refined
through continued review and critique, which has expanded the
definition and application of its claims. Some concluded that the
original five levels were not exhaustive and have since added
additional levels to the hierarchy. Others have contended that
more than one need can motivate an individual at any given time,

resulting in them having the ability to move through the levels more fluidly than originally believed. Regardless of the interpretation, one sentiment remains constant throughout each of Maslow's levels, that is *satisfying personal needs is humanity's greatest motivator.*

Maslow doesn't allocate motivational currency to meeting needs in general but distinctively to meeting personal needs. His theory implies that we progress from being motivated to meet our most self-sustaining (level 1) needs of food and shelter to being motivated to meet our most self-fulfilling (level 5) needs of achievement and proficiency. Either way, it is all about SELF. Even when we are seeking to satisfy the needs of a relationship and intimacy with others, the primary motivator is not to meet that need for the person(s) we are in relationship with, it is to meet our personal need to be in relationship with others.

Each level of the hierarchy excludes the needs of others, which suggests that personal needs are intrinsically humanity's greatest motivator, both in terms of *priority* and *portion*. Priority determines the order of importance something has and portion determines the amount of importance, or influence, something has. So, the connotation is that our personal needs are so powerful that we, as human beings, are naturally motivated to meet them before being motivated to doing anything else and that meeting our personal needs continuously motivates our behavior more than anything else, including the needs of others.

To be clear, it's not just having personal needs that is the greatest influence of our motives, it's the unyielding internal urge to meet them that naturally dictates our behavior. If we adopt Maslow's theory, then this point of meeting personal needs being our greatest motivator is key to understanding why we generally define fulfillment or success the way we do. Attaining success is a prominent force in our lives because, whether consciously or subconsciously, we have aligned our personal needs with success; specifically, we have defined success as the meeting of our personal needs. For example, if you need food and you get it, then you've attained a level of success; if you need protection and you find it, then you've attained more success; if you need respect and you earn it, then you've attained an even higher level of success. As we move up the hierarchy, we continuously reframe our understanding of success as meeting all of our personal needs on that level.

Being an objective person, I understand that much debate can be had on this point. One could argue that this is an overly generalized interpretation and application of Maslow's claims and that most people who ascribe to his theory of motivation wouldn't define success as the meeting of their personal needs. I would argue that if Maslow's list holds true, then all of our motives stem from self-satisfaction through the meeting of personal needs. For instance, he doesn't put "feed others" as a need for level 1 or "increase the esteem of others" as a need for level 4. I would then denote that the source of our motives drives our objectives and that the meeting of those objectives produce our feelings of success. Put this way, it would be safe to say that we define success as the ability to appease our motives through accomplishment; and when solely motivated to meet our ever-evolving personal needs, we are inevitably inclined to center our efforts on fulfillment of self rather than service to others.

· · ·

Complication

To be clear, I don't believe that Maslow was proposing that we, as humans, care nothing about the needs of others. You would be hard-pressed to find a mother who isn't concerned with the needs of her child or a nurse unmoved by the dire requests of his or her patients. However, I do think that there are two possible assumptions that can be made about meeting others' needs based on the sole inclusion of personal needs in the hierarchy. One assumption is that personal needs must be met before we can be motivated to help meet the needs of others; the other is that helping to meet the needs of others is tied to the meeting of our personal needs.

The first assumption is pretty self-explanatory, it's the thought or belief that "I have to do for myself before I am able to do for others"; that I have to first be satisfied in order to serve. The second assumption, on the other hand, is a bit more cryptic, so I'll explain further. If the satisfaction of your personal needs for belongingness, or self-esteem, or self-actualization require – based on your internal feelings of fulfillment – that you help to meet the needs of others, similar to the mother/child and nurse/patient examples, then in order to have that personal need met, you must contribute to meeting the need(s) of another. So, at the core, it's not really about helping others, it is about you. By tying their needs to yours, you are making the fulfillment of theirs the means to ultimately fulfilling yours.

Though both of these assumptions are understandable and well-meaning, they are problematic in the pursuit and completion of your purpose. The primary issue does not lie with Maslow's theory because, all things considered, it is riddled with truth. The issue lies with the manifested implications of his theory, which is that all of our pursuits are grounded in self. We either feel we must fulfill self before we are able to serve others or we only serve others when it's connected to our personal feelings of fulfillment. Simply put, any motivation we may have to serve the needs of others is rooted in self-fulfillment.

When your service to others is dependent on self-fulfillment, then you will never complete your purpose! Why, you ask? Because true service – the type of service that enables purpose to effectively operate by pouring out resources to connect divinity to humanity – is delivered through self-sacrifice and is destroyed by self-fulfillment as its intent. **You cannot provide the world what you were created to give if you are timing it with or tying it to your unmet personal needs.** I say "unmet" personal needs because the reality is, your personal needs will never be 100% met. As seasons change in your life – heck, even as the days change – you will always be in abundance in one area, or moment, and lacking in another. You will have plenty of money but lack in companionship or have a gratifying job but depleting health. You'll go from stuffed to famished, from safety to insecurity, from loved to neglected, confident to low-esteem, and on and on...it never ends. As your life is cyclical, so are your needs! Therefore, if your service is contingent on all your personal needs being satisfied, then your purpose will be compelling to discuss and post about, but will never be completed.

Many people have allowed their personal needs to disable them from executing their purpose. They either excuse their *lack* of service by telling themselves that they have to be at a certain point of self-fulfillment (i.e. mentally, emotionally, financially, socially, etc.) before they can serve others, or they excuse their *limitation* of service to others by reducing it down to the point where they feel their personal needs are met, instead of extending it to the point where the needs of those they are serving are met.

Solution

Purpose is given to you by your Creator and thus can be realized, but not changed. Success, on the other hand, is dependent on how you define it. Since the *Why* of your purpose is your life's objective, success shouldn't be defined by the meeting of personal needs, rather it should be defined by whether or not you have met, or are meeting, the objective of your purpose. The truth is, how you define success will ultimately determine how you pursue it, how you measure it, and how you judge the outputs/fruits of your efforts to attain it.

If you define success as the meeting of your personal needs then you will ultimately align your pursuits in life toward self-fulfilling things. You will erroneously measure your level of success in life by how many personal needs and desires you've been able to meet, only feeling successful when you seemingly need fewer things. Furthermore, you will wrongfully assess the value of your labor based on how much it profits your life, thinking your effort is only valuable if its outputs benefit you.

Now, let's turn the coin over and examine the other side. If you define success as the completion of your life's objective, then you will align your pursuits toward objective, or purpose, fulfilling things. You will measure your level of success by how many divine connections you are able to make and how many avenues, or *Whats*, you are able to pour from. Additionally, using an impact-driven definition of success, you'll rightfully determine the value of your work based on how much it produces in the life of others; believing your effort matters when it improves your surroundings, and hopefully, the world at large. This is the ideal definition of success to operate from because your aim should not be completing God's job of meeting all your own needs, instead, it should be to meet your life's objective!

By understanding success in this context, you can easily draw a correlation between your definition of success and your perspective of purpose. Whatever you deem your mission in life to be, your assessed level of success will be based on how much of that mission you've completed. Put another way, your understanding of purpose will inform your definition of success and that definition will ultimately drive or motivate your decision-making and actions. Therefore, in order to change the source of your motives from self to service, you must redefine success as the completion of purpose rather than the meeting of personal needs.

Application

The need to redefine success is a concept that is easy to accept but hard to execute. Once you've become aware that you need to change the way you think about success, accepting that reality is fairly easy because I think, for the most part, people have a genuine desire to mature and evolve into more awakened, self-aware versions of themselves. It's usually when our existing value systems fail us – when we actually attain what we've been pursuing but it doesn't bring us satisfaction – that we realize we need to redefine our ideas of success and place our values into more satisfying and impactful things. The key questions that surface when we experience these types of revelation-induced growth spurts are *"what should I start placing my values in?"* and *"how do I start doing it?"*

You found out in the Solution section of this chapter that you have to start putting your values into fulfilling the objective of your purpose, instead of putting them into fulfilling your personal needs and desires. This is because satisfaction doesn't come from gathering the things you don't have, rather it is realized when you intentionally disperse or pour out the resources you do have! The question that remains, is "how?" *How do I stop using the fulfillment of self to define success for my life?* Now, it may seem counterintuitive, but the way to start valuing self-fulfillment less is to begin to value yourself more. I know it sounds a bit crazy, but let me provide an example, and hopefully, it will help to clarify!

When I was in high school, I wanted absolutely nothing more than to play on my school's basketball team! I would say "to play varsity" but honestly, I would have been just as thrilled to have made my Freshman or Junior Varsity (J.V.) teams as well. As you can probably guess from my expression of desperation, I didn't make the Freshman team in my first year and was once again cut as a sophomore from the J.V. squad.

Despite my previous failures, I doubled down in the off-season between my sophomore and junior years in pure determination to make Varsity that winter. I played on the school's spring and summer league teams to improve my pace of play and joined the cross-country team (neither of which had tryouts, thank God), running 5 to 8 miles every day after school just to improve my endurance for basketball. I went to my neighborhood basketball court early every morning that summer to work on my shooting and dribbling skills.

To sweeten the pot, I ran into the assistant Varsity coach at the court one morning, before he met with another player, and convinced him to show me some drills to practice, which I did for the rest of the summer. At tryouts that year, no one could touch me...I knew I was going to make the team! I was one of the first to finish in each running drill and went toe-to-toe with the best players every scrimmage. I pushed to out-work all the other players because I wanted to make the team more than anybody on the court and I had the endurance to prove it. After three grueling days of tryouts, I once again had to face the demoralizing feeling of scouring the coveted list of selected team members that didn't have my name on it.

After I collected myself and received the consolation pats on the back from my friends who had made the team, and even those who didn't, I talked with the coach to find out why. He explained that he had seen me come a long way, but his existing team already knew the system. They had been playing with each other for years and unless I was a super exceptional talent, he was going with his core guys.

Well, you would think that would be enough for me, but this was a self-actualized need of mine and I had made up in my mind that I was going to get what I wanted by making the team my senior year! So, a few days later, I came back to him and asked if I could be the team manager, a.k.a. the "water/laundry/equipment/get talked about in your face and behind your back" boy. Knowing that I was friends with most of the team, the coach asked why I would want that position. I explained to him that if it was not knowing the plays and not being a part of the unit that kept me from making the team, this would be my way of meeting those requirements. I figured since the manager had to be at every practice and game, then I would learn the system and hopefully step in for anyone who missed practice so I could play and gel with the guys. Plus, it would show him how bad I wanted it and the level of effort I'd be willing to put in. After he gave me the disclaimer that it would not guarantee me a spot on next year's team, the coach accepted my proposal and I made what, at the time, was the worst decision I had ever made!

It was already bad enough having to do the stuff I knew about before taking the position, like filling water bottles and gathering basketballs and cones after practice, but the stuff I didn't know about made it ten times worse! I didn't know I had to collect and wash the sweaty funky practice and game jerseys, not to mention having to cart them through the school hallways between periods from the laundry room to the locker room on opposite sides of the school. Those who were fortunate enough to witness this sight quickly spread the word and I was talked about like I didn't have ears! I didn't know I had to dress up for the games, so in case you attended a game and weren't sure if I was the manager or not, you were able to easily find out because warm-ups were for the players and I was the only young person in a shirt and tie. I also didn't know that people pay attention to the sidelines just as much as the game, so the players' parents and the girls in school knew me as "the manager".

Side Note: *There is nothing worse than feeling like you're good enough to play on the team and introducing yourself to someone only to hear them say "yeah, I know you, you're the manager, right?"*

Regardless of how I felt about my position, the harsh reality was that I was good at it. I am abnormally organized, so all of the equipment was well accounted for, stored, and maintained. Part of my chores at home was doing laundry for all five of us, so not only were the jerseys fresh, it was light work for me. I was always good at math, so recording stats was a breeze, I even analyzed some of them to help provide the coaches with detailed information. In addition to all of that, I learned all the plays and the players like the back of my hand!

The point of this story is partially to entertain you with one of the darkest times in my high school career (you're welcome), but more so to show you that the process of redefining success requires you to stop looking outside of yourself, valuing what you don't have, and to start looking inside of yourself to value all you do have!

At that time in my life, success for me – like it is for most of us – was doing and getting what I wanted, which in this case was to make the team. Like the rest of the players who didn't have to check the list to know they made it, if I was already on the team, my pursuit of success would likely be focused on obtaining something else I hadn't yet accomplished. Though it was frustrating to endure, being the manager of the team helped me realize the resources that were already inside of me by redirecting my attention from only trying to gain the things that weren't. I'm sure I would've scored some points, made some nice assists and grabbed a few rebounds (had the coach ever put me in the games) while playing on the team, but looking back, I served that group so much more as a manager than I ever could as a player.

I can't point to a specific time, but I am sure serving as the manager of the Massaponax High Varsity Basketball Team was the inception of the shift in my understanding of success. **Over the years, I have worked to redefine success to be the intentional and effective disbursement of my characteristics, capabilities, and qualities. The more ways I can improve a person, community, or situation using the gifts and abilities at my disposal, the more successful I believe I am.** The only way you can get to that point is if you first take an inventory of the valuable things within you, of which you have an endless supply!

You have to do what I suggested earlier in this section, which is to start thinking of yourself more! In other words, you have to get to know yourself on a deeper level, a level beyond your desires, where your God-given treasures reside. People who are only aware of or are only concerned with what they're missing have no choice but to define success through self-fulfillment; they can only value what they have to gain because they are either unaware of or don't value what they have to give!

In case you're wondering, even though I killed it in tryouts the next year, I didn't make the basketball team as a senior either. The coach felt he needed to make room for the young guys to maintain continuity after the seniors left. If I didn't know it before, I definitely gained a sense of it after I got cut the fourth year in a row – you can't control whether or not you get what you want in life, so it's faulty logic to base your definition of success on getting the things you don't have. The only way you can determine if you're successful is by whether or not you effectively manage (pun intended) the few things you do have control of! You can decide if you are going to identify and value your resources, you can decide if you're going to pour out those resources to serve others, and you can decide if you are going to define your success in life based on that service. If it's your desire to redefine success in this manner, complete these practical yet necessary steps:

1. **Take an Inventory:** Ask yourself and those close to you what your resources (i.e. characteristics, capabilities, and qualities) are that currently, or potentially could, benefit others and then list them on a piece of paper.

2. **Assess the Value:** Write your personal feelings about each of the items on the list to assess the level of value you place on it. This step is simply for awareness; try to open yourself up to utilizing a resource that you currently place a low value on, but can potentially have a high impact for others (i.e. executing team manager duties).

3. **Intentionally Pour:** Find one to three different avenues, areas, places, etc. you can apply one or more

of those resources in a way that benefits someone or something other than just yourself.

4. **Journal:** Document your effort and then reassess to see if your perspective and understanding of success has started to shift.

Chapter 5

FROM GAIN TO GIVE

SHIFT THE STEPS OF YOUR MOTIVATION

T he second dimension of your motivation that we will address is its *steps*/its resulting actions. It's asking yourself the question "what steps/actions am I being motivated to take?" To help enhance the contrast between the first dimension (source) of your motivation and the second (steps), allow me to use the analogy of a tree. If your motivation is the tree trunk and the branches, then the source is the root and the steps are the fruit. The root feeds your motives and the fruit is what your motives produce. Therefore, your steps/actions are the tangible and measurable outputs of your motives.

As detailed in the previous chapter, there is an intrinsic source of "self" that feeds our motivations as humans. Likewise, in our actions, we have natural inclinations that are outputs of our source. When self is the source of our motives, we are inherently motivated to "gain" rather than to "give", in order to achieve the self-fulfillment we desire.

Maslow's Hierarchy of Needs helped to provide an understanding of why we naturally seek to meet personal needs over the needs of others in order to attain fulfillment. We uncovered that our sense of fulfillment is tied to our definition of success and if we can redefine success for our lives then we can operate from a mindset that aims to fulfill purpose through service, rather than to fulfill self. Transforming the source of our motivation is righteous, yet the right motivation in the wrong direction will still lead to failure! That said, if we are going to live out the best version of our lives by completing our purpose, in addition to correcting the source of our motivation, we also have to address the actions we are motivated to take.

Delving into the *gain* and *give* actions will help us to better understand how we, as humans, innately go about trying to obtain the personal fulfillment we inherently seek. It makes sense that if we are naturally motivated by our own needs to be fulfilled, then we would also be naturally inclined to meet those needs by gaining what we don't have rather than giving what we do have. Many of us operate from a "gain" approach that tells us we have to get as much as we can in order to meet our personal needs and ultimately be fulfilled in life. It's a belief that the way to a better life is by acquiring all that our heart desires. However, purpose-fulfillment requires us to flip the script and function from a "give" approach to fulfillment, where we not only look to serve the need(s) of others, but to do so through our giving.

It may not seem like it, but it is possible for you to be motivated by a service mindset, yet be motivated to gain rather than give. An example of this would be someone whose creativity and passion is ignited by the plight of others (e.g., broken marriages, poverty, racial injustices, etc.) but they will only pour for the

right price (e.g., honorariums, book advances, rider requirements, etc.). Those in this column require to gain something
before they feel it's feasible or worth it to start pouring out their
resources to serve the external needs they are driven to meet.
Being able to adopt a "give" approach will enable you to recog-
nize and overcome the ever-present excuses that are currently
keeping you from completing your purpose. You may not have
everything you want (e.g. money, time, experience, and knowledge) to fill the gaps you were created and are motivated to fill,
at the level and magnitude you desire to fill them, however, you
do have everything you need to make an impact right where you
are, you just have to pour!

When you make giving your approach to fulfilling your
purpose, then you will be free to flow, free from preconditions,
from prerequisites, and from pre-qualifications of status or
circumstance. Your pour will be predicated on access to your
divine resources (provision) rather than acquisition of your
divine requests (answered prayers) to gain from and/or for what
you give. For lasting transformation to take place, in order for
you to become who you were purposed and created to be, it's
imperative that you not only shift the source of your motives
from self to service, but that you also shift the steps you are
being motivated to take, from gaining to giving!

Inclination

When I was younger, I was always intrigued by movies and
shows with genies in them; the two movies that come to mind
are *Kazaam* and *Aladdin*. After watching one, I remember me

and my brothers used to share what our three wishes would be if ever prompted by a genie who was willing to give us anything we wanted. It was rare that we would say anything that didn't include making our lives better in some way. If we were feeling really generous, we would try to get everything we wanted in the first two wishes and reserve the last one for a Miss America-type request like realizing world peace or ending world hunger.

One answer that never made its way to our lips was wishing to lose or lessen something that we already had. I never would ask a genie to take away my video games, or shoes, or TV. It wasn't necessarily because I had a high value on those things – I would play outside in my sneakers and slap the TV when it wasn't doing what I wanted – it was because I placed so much value on the things I hadn't yet attained. I mean, why would I waste a perfectly good wish on taking something away rather than putting it to better use by adding something I didn't have? The truth is, I wouldn't! And I'm willing to bet that you wouldn't either. I don't know what your wishes would be – perhaps they would be for more money, more recognition, better health, increased intellect, or something else that's not easily attained but seemingly worth having. **The point is that we rarely if ever attribute giving to good living. Sure, we feel good when we give, but we don't believe it is the path to success and fulfillment. If anything, it is something that we believe that attaining a certain level of success will afford us.**

Don't get me wrong, though I respect the movement, I am not a minimalist nor am I advocating for you to become one; I like getting stuff like the next person. My goal is to provide a source of reflection when it comes to your pursuit of what you deem success to be, in light of fulfilling your purpose on earth. We already know, from the previous chapter, why we are naturally convicted to satisfy the needs of self over the needs of others, but now we are clear on how we inherently go about doing it. We instinctively try to meet our needs in order to succeed and we attempt to do it by gaining things we don't have. Our "gain" mentality causes us to look out into the world and identify all the things – all the opportunities, all the experiences, all the connections, and all the items – that we have a desire for but are not currently in possession of. This approach is not concerned with personal needs that have been met because that is seemingly a misutilization of resources; it is only aware of and constantly in pursuit of what's missing from our lives. The reality is, we wouldn't use our wishes to give something up, not because we are selfish and self-centered people, but because it's easier to see and pursue the things we are without rather than the things we have within us!

Complication

The issue with attempting to achieve success through gain is that it redirects your attention away from purpose and toward possession. When your mind becomes focused on gaining what you're missing then, in my 70's black preacher voice, your eyes and energy become fixated on *"what you're lacking instead of what you're packing!"* It's like when the genie asks the person what they wish for, the only things that come to their mind – when looking across the landscape of their lives – are the things they value but don't have in their possession! The lack in your life, which is everything you think you should or could have but currently don't, becomes very evident and takes priority when operating from a gain approach. As such, that lack often functions as the incubator for your unquenched desires and fuels your undying drive to gain more and more. In a nutshell, **your *lack* negatively affects your *look*!** If you are solely, or even primarily, driven by the desire to satiate your lack, it will significantly distort your out**look** on life.

A distorted outlook crosses your vision and causes you to see yourself and the world around you in an inverted manner. Purpose intends for you to see the fullness of resources that are within you and the gaping needs that exist around you, in the people and places you're connected to. Yet, because your outlook is distorted by your lack, you only see the needs or gaps present within yourself, and in a mirage-type fashion, you see the fullness of resources that are deceptively present in the world around you. You are therefore unable to achieve purposeful success by pouring from your abundance of internal resources to fill external gaps because your aim is to achieve personal possession by gaining external things in an attempt to fill your internal gaps.

In addition to altering your outlook to only seeing your lack, a focused pursuit on gain will also negatively impact your ability to effectively assess your development. You will start to confuse obtaining with progressing; believing that when you get more, you have accomplished more and have become a better version of yourself. Though obtaining and progressing are not mutually exclusive, they are also not the same thing. You can obtain things while you progress in life but your progress is not predicated on your ability to obtain things or how much you have obtained. Just because you're gaining doesn't mean you're growing, nor does it mean you are successfully completing your purpose!

The last major detriment to operating from a gain mindset is that it will also cause you to rely on false evidence to validate your true worth. This touches on the sentiments expressed in our Attribute of "Matter" from Chapter 1. When it comes to assessing our worth in a particular area or discipline, and ultimately in life, many of us generally base it on what we have gained. In other words, we tend to rely on the value of the tangible and intangible things we've either obtained (received) or attained (achieved) to prove that we are valuable and that we matter. For some, it's the value of the tangible things (houses, cars, assets, etc.) they've gained that determines their worth. For others, it's the value of the intangible things (i.e. knowledge, influence, status, etc.) they've amassed that indicates their worth. Yet true worth is not validated by what something or someone obtains or attains from the outside-in, only by what they produce and provide from the inside-out!

Steve Jobs' worth was not validated by the billions he obtained – Forbes has a whole list of people who are billionaires many times over – it was validated by the world-changing ideas and innovation he produced. The worth of a diamond is not validated by the minerals and elements that go into it, but rather for the beauty, luster, and shine that emits from it. A tree is not made valid by how much sun it is able to get or how much water it can obtain, it's worth is determined and is validated by what it renders to others (e.g. fruit, oxygen, shade, etc.). Likewise, your worth cannot be validated and your impact is not made by what you gain from this world; your worth is established at conception and is validated by what you produce in and ultimately give to this world.

Solution

Let's assume that you were totally convinced by my argument in the last section and you now agree that using gain to achieve success and fulfillment is a faulty and fruitless approach. Well, welcome aboard! Yet, despite being a believer, I'm willing to bet that you're still not 100% onboard with this whole giving thing; that you're still skeptical about how giving will lead to fulfillment. If you're anything like me, I'm sure there's a rational, pragmatic part of you that's wondering "so, what's in it for me?"

Unfamiliarity breeds uncertainty within each of us and, therefore, that part of you that thrives on practicality is likely posing fear-provoked questions such as "if I am making personal sacrifices to meet the needs of others, through my giving, how will I be taken care of?", "How will I progress in life?", "What will I have for myself?", "When and in what way will I get a return on my efforts?" These types of questions are more than valid as they are innate to our self-preserving human instincts for survival.

On every flight I've been on, before taking-off, all of the passengers are instructed by the attendants to, in an emergency situation, put on their own oxygen mask before helping other passengers with putting theirs on. I used to wonder why they had to tell people that. It almost seemed like a "duh" thing to say, I mean, who in their right mind would make sure someone else can breathe before being able to breathe themselves?

> **Side Note:** *This is before I became a husband and father. It now makes complete sense that, as the protector of my family, I would attempt to put my daughter's and wife's masks on them before I put on my own!*

This was my initial reaction because we as humans have a natural inclination to **only** give to others out of our overflow, not out of our lack. Therefore, it was relatively common sense for me to think that only breathing people, those with plenty of oxygen, would be willing and able to help someone else to also breathe. Whether you're aware of it or not, this sentiment is likely exhibited in your current approach to giving. Chances are, you're only willing to volunteer in your free time, or donate money after you pay your bills and set aside some "rainy day" funds, or do favors for people once your work and personal responsibilities are first taken care of. It's not that you aren't willing to give of yourself, it's that your common sense tells you that you have to attain a level of sufficiency and/or satisfaction in order to give or do for others; that you have to have your mask on before helping the person next to you put theirs on.

Given the direction of this book, you probably think that I am about to try and reverse your thinking to convince you to start giving out of, or in spite of, your lack, but you'd be wrong. Very much in line with the old adage that "you can't pour from an empty cup", I actually agree that we should give to others from our abundance, which I try to maintain as a staple in my own life! What I do want to bring to light though are two common misconceptions regarding what your abundance is and where your abundance comes from.

The first misconception is that your giving supply – or the things you give to others in service – should come from your overflow instead of your abundance. Now, on the surface, these two things appear to be the same, but as it relates to your giving, they're not. **"Overflow" speaks to the level of supply you have attained and "Abundance" details the level of supply you have access to!** This distinction makes a huge difference in your willingness and ability to give in the fulfillment of your purpose. Reason being, many of us – as alluded to in the previous examples of time, money, and energy depicted above – innately only give from our overflow. However, the depth and weight of your purpose requires that you instead give from your abundance!

Overflow giving says, "I am giving these shoes to someone in need because I have two other pairs just like them and don't have enough space in my closet to store them." Abundance giving says, "I am giving these shoes to someone in need because my parents own an apparel company and I get new shoes all the time!" Notice the difference in the reasons for giving. The impetus for giving from overflow is your deficiency; you give because you lack the capacity, the desire, or the personal need to maintain the supply you have amassed. Conversely, the catalyst for giving from abundance is the deficiency or present need of another. Herein lies the issue with giving from your overflow – especially in the fulfillment of your purpose. It forces you to focus on your inventory of supply more than the need(s) you were created to meet! In other words, overflow giving directs your energy and efforts toward trying to increase and maintain your supply; to getting more shoes and more closet space rather than giving more shoes to those without them.

Now, you may be saying, "Merrick, I hear you but that's not me! I don't just give from the overage of things I can't maintain. I am being motivated to give in order to meet needs!" If that's you then great, I am truly happy for you and encourage you to continue to do so. That said, I do want to address one more misconception about where the abundance of your giving supply comes from.

As I mentioned before, you don't have the capacity nor the ability to fill yourself, you can only choose to empty yourself! That said, it is not your job, but rather the job of your divine Source to fill you (i.e. provide your giving supply) via a connection with Him. He fills you in a number of ways; sometimes it's directly with *intangible provisions* like love, joy, peace, and hope, which **fuels** you in your giving. Other times, He fills you indirectly through *tangible provisions*, like money, connections, and opportunities (or an endless supply of shoes) from the people He intentionally and strategically places in your life, which **equips** you for your giving. In other words, the problem is not you wanting to give from your abundance, it's you wanting to create the abundance that you give from!

In reference to our airplane example, instead of putting on your mask and then looking to help others with theirs, you are busy trying to create the oxygen supply. You, like many people, have adopted a skewed perspective that sees the creation of your abundance as your duty and giving, or pouring out, as your gift to others. **The truth is, God's abundance is your GIFT from Him and giving/pouring out to others is your intended DUTY!**

It's in this revelation that we find the validity of our need to approach the fulfillment of our purpose through giving rather than through gain. When our intended duty of giving becomes optional – whether because it's dependent on us having more than enough (overflow) or because it's dependent on us producing the supply (abundance creation) – then the intended results of that duty, which is fulfillment of purpose, cannot be realized. When giving to others in the fulfillment of purpose becomes your duty or mission, then not only will your purpose be fulfilled but your concerns about "what's in it for me?" will start to dissipate. Only those who attempt to create abundance worry about where it will come from and how it will get to them. On the other hand, receivers of abundance only worry about where it will go and how to get it there!

Receivers of abundance function like open drains in a bathtub, with God's supply being the water filling up the tub. As long as the drain remains unplugged and provides a place for the water in the tub to be emptied, then the water in the tub will keep rushing to the drain and the faucet will stay on, continuing to supply more and more water because it has a place to flow. Simply put, **abundance goes where abundance flows!** You can't control how much water will go into your tub, that's the faucet's (i.e. God's) job. However, you can control how much of the water will be emptied out of your tub. One thing is for sure, closed drains result in backed up tubs, which eventually requires the faucet to be shut off and the water to be capped at the capacity of the tub - this is true in your bathroom and in your life!

On the surface, it looks like your dependence on the provision of an outside source is binding and will restrict you to only going as far as your source will allow. Having that level of dependence on something or someone other than ourselves creates real fear in many of us. Therefore, we attempt to relieve that fear by taking matters into our own hands and working to produce our own supply. In essence, we have equated independence to freedom, believing that when we are self-sustained, we are free from limits; free from limits on our income, limits on our impact, and limits on our improvement. On the contrary, **choosing to give from your provided supply, rather than trying to create your own independent supply in the fulfillment of purpose, is not bondage but true freedom! It's freedom from the shackles of your personal limitations!**

Pouring from your Source's endless supply, rather than your restricted one, frees you to pursue dreams bigger than the limits of self. I'm sure this goes without saying, but just for emphasis, let me remind you that YOU ARE HUMAN! And as a human, you can only operate within the boundaries of your personal limitations. **The limits of your energy, knowledge, language, money, tolerance, and so on will be your prison rather than your starting point.**

Developing a dependency on God, as your limitless source, frees you to execute a purpose that requires ideas that are far greater than your experience and mental aptitude can produce, services that go beyond the peak of your capabilities and capacities, and connections that expand farther than your language barriers and level of influence! Giving can only become missional when you start intentionally distributing your **provided** supply and stop trying to offer the supply you've **manufactured** but can't maintain! Making this transition will free you to accomplish much more with what you've been gifted than you ever could with what you've gained.

Application

At this point, it is my sincere hope that I have presented a strong enough case to convince you – or at least cause you to reconsider – the purpose-fulfilling power of your giving. That your conscience has been awakened to the revelation that, when it comes to fulfilling purpose, we not only need to make the meeting of other's needs the motivation for our efforts (Service Mindset), but also that those efforts must not be to gain from our service, but to give through our service (Give Approach). In order to be able to make this shift, you found that…

1. As detailed in Chapter 4 - You have to alter your definition of success (i.e. your primary motivator) from meeting personal needs to completing your purpose.
2. As detailed in this chapter - You have to alter your approach to success from treating giving as your gift to the world, to making it your life's duty/mission in the world.

Though we have gone into depth about why this transition of

your approach to fulfilling your purpose is key, the question that remains is "How?" How do you transition your giving from being your gift to becoming your duty?

The short answer is to start giving out of necessity instead of nicety. Simply put, **give because you have to, not because you want to!** The thing about giving is that it has universally been regarded as a righteous pursuit. That those who are good (e.g., those who are pure in heart, intention, and action) are the ones who give to those in need. This sentiment is supported and perpetuated by stories such as *A Christmas Carol*, where Mr. Scrooge has a change of heart and goes from being greedy to generous as a tangible sign of his transformation from bad to good. Willy Wonka gives his chocolate factory to a poor boy named Charlie to reveal his true character after being viewed by everyone as a disconnected, insensitive candy maker. At the end of *The Color Purple*, Mister succumbs to the perils of Celie's curse on his life and, in turn, is awakened to the error of his ways; the audience sees this internal change evidenced in his act of kindness by paying for Celie to be reunited with her long-lost children.

In each of these dramatized examples, and in many more throughout our society, giving – especially to those with a lesser lot in life – is seen as an indicator of moral standing. Yes, it's nice to give, especially to those who are in need, however, purpose sees giving in a completely different light. **Purpose doesn't just recommend or respect giving; it requires giving!** The purpose of a light bulb is to give light; the purpose of a bike is to give rides; the purpose of a ball is to give recreation, and the purpose of a human being is to give resources to other humans.

If you are waiting on your moral compass to point to "give" before you feel compelled to offer your abundance, then fulfilling your purpose will remain a desire but never become a reality. To make giving a necessity in your life, you have to remove the fluid and fleeting driver of feelings (e.g., sympathy, guilt, etc.) and replace them with the consistent driver of fulfillment. Feelings are the biggest detriment to giving because they make something that is lasting (giving) reliant on something that is temporary (emotions).

The greatest givers are those who give FOR a result, not those who give AS a result. Those who only give as a result of something unintended taking place are only moved by moments. They have to be in the right mood or have all the right vibes before they are motivated to execute the primary requirement of their purpose, which is to give! The purpose business – much like a store's supply chain with its manufacturers, distributors, and retail locations – is a heavily dependent enterprise. You are dependent on God as your resource supplier and others are dependent on your distribution of resources to meet their needs. A successful store can't pick and choose when to transfer its goods based on emotional status; likewise, your purpose's interconnected reliance on the transfer of life-changing supply is too demanding to be completed through reactionary, unintended giving. Therefore, you have to give to produce an intended result!

Giving for intended results is simply the planned transfer of resources to produce a predetermined outcome. Bill and Melinda Gates give to eradicate major world diseases; Oprah gives to provide high-level education to children in Africa; Tony Robbins gives to end hunger in America. Planned actions and predetermined outcomes aren't birthed out of moods, but out of necessity – the necessity for impact to be made and destiny realized.

Question: Is there a predetermined outcome that your giving has to – not just wants to or possibly could – produce in the world? A gap it has to fill? If so, what are you doing to make sure that it will?

As I alluded to, the way to start giving out of necessity to produce an intended outcome is to plan for it! Many of us, when we think of planning our giving, think of setting aside a certain amount of money in our budget to give to a church, a charity, or another worthy cause. Though that is part of it, it's not all of it! Intentional giving – giving to fulfill your life's purpose – is holistic and goes beyond the planned allocation of your monetary funds. This type of giving is not just from what you have, but for what you have been put on earth to complete. Therefore, in addition to your money, it also requires you to plan out the activities, the time, and the effort necessary for your giving to accomplish all it is intended to accomplish. See, **when your giving is deconstructed into activities (actionable steps) and has time and energy allocated to it, then it is way more likely to be executed based on your one constant purpose rather than your many changing feelings and moods!**

There are a few practical steps you can take to plan out your giving in a way that will produce its intended outcome. One step is to sit down with your calendar and schedule brainstorming sessions (individual sessions or group sessions with those connected to your life/purpose) to identify ways you can pour out to others in the fulfillment of your purpose. This will help you to trim the fat of stuff that would be "nice to do" and start to hone in on the key areas you can pour into that will create the most positive change. Perhaps there are established organizations you can plug into, opportunities at your job, etc. that are at your disposal and need the resources you have to offer.

Once you have come up with some ideas, you can continue that same scheduling process to plan out the dates and times you will execute those activities. This is the point where holistic giving will require your planning to go a step further. In addition to putting the necessary activities on a calendar/schedule, you will need to also consider and plan for the amount of funds, level of effort, and quantity of time required to execute those activities at the level necessary to produce the predetermined outcome. In practice, this is done by making sure you provide yourself adequate time to personally (e.g., physically, mentally, emotionally, and spiritually), relationally, and financially prepare for and recover from your scheduled giving activities. For example, don't plan a 12-hour volunteer effort the day before a big presentation at work, or spend your spouse's birthday with your mentee without their prior consent, or donate large sums of money to a fundraising campaign right after emptying the majority of your life savings for the down payment on your new house!

Remember the goal of your giving is not to drain you, but to fulfill your purpose! If we are going to redirect our giving to produce intended outcomes, then the focus can no longer be on what we are giving but rather on what we are producing from our giving! When it comes to giving, many people want credit for how much time, energy, money, and so forth that they gave, with little to no focus on what came from their efforts. If you have filled up your schedule with giving activities but are offering minimal effort and attention, or producing little to no impact while completing the activities, then you have elevated the giving over the outcome. Adequately planning your giving will help you to bring your full self (i.e., your resources, effort, and time) to the giving activity so that it will produce a needed impact rather than a nice gesture.

As you plan and execute your giving, be sure to track it as well! This is a key step because tracking your giving will enable you to look back and see if it is producing what it is intended to produce. If you are trying to end hunger in America, but instead your efforts are clothing more people than feeding them, then you need to adjust your giving. These adjustments can only be made by adequately tracking the outcomes of your giving efforts. You can do this by simply taking count of quantities where you can; noting how many people came to the event, how much money was collected, how many meals were prepared, how many people were fed, etc.

Another way to track progress and improve your giving is to survey the people you are aiming to serve! You can use surveys/questionnaires to first find out what their needs specifically are. Yes, they may be hungry, but they may not have the means to store and prepare food so they need ready-made meals, not groceries. As you aim to meet those needs through your giving, you can then use surveys/questionnaires again to follow-up in order to see if their needs are adequately being met or not. This is where many people stumble in their giving when it comes to fulfilling purpose; they blindly give with no insight into impact. People who give to a demographic with no insight into the needs or opinions of that demographic are giving to feel good, not to produce an outcome that makes a purposed change, which is what your giving must do!

I am more than confident that if you adequately plan out and effectively execute your giving activities, you will successfully implement an approach to intentional giving that enables you to complete your purpose! In your pursuit to fulfill purpose, it's necessary to adopt a mindset that motivates you to serve the needs of others through your giving. This type of God-directed work is easy to comprehend and even to start, but like with any other challenging endeavor in life (e.g., diet, exercise, therapy, etc.) that produces desired results, it is one that is very difficult to maintain over a meaningful period of time. To be able to accomplish this cumbersome effort you have to establish and pay attention to indicators that will alert you when you are sliding back into personal fulfillment and getting away from purpose-fulfillment. The same way we monitor weight gain to know when we need to get back in the gym or outbursts of anger to know we need to schedule another appointment with our therapist, we also have to monitor the signs of mis-motivation.

Chapter 6

FROM POOR TO POUR

SHIFT THE SIGNS OF YOUR MOTIVATION

M otivation with the wrong source and/or wrong steps (i.e. mis-motivation) makes the completion of purpose an impossibility. When it comes to fulfillment, you cannot be both the pitcher and the cup – the benefactor of your pour and the beneficiary of your pour. When you are motivated to be one, then you negate the requirements and responsibilities that it takes to be the other. Likewise, you cannot aim to fulfill both self and purpose simultaneously; one is always going to take a backseat to the other and it's for this reason we have to know when we have stopped pursuing one and started to pursue the other. We need to be aware of the signs that indicate the true source and steps of our motives so we can adjust when and where needed to ensure we not only start but maintain a mindset that consistently produces purpose-completing actions.

There are many indicators that we could take into consideration when trying to determine whether we are focused on fulfilling ourselves or our purpose. We could take into account all the superficial things that we as humans usually assess when trying to determine if we are accomplishing our goals or not – tracking things like how many people are supporting our efforts, the magnitude of the results we are producing compared to others, or the amount of work we are putting into our desired outcomes. Yet, in order to identify the right indicators for purpose-fulfillment, you have to get back to the heart, or the *Why*, of your purpose, which is to facilitate Heaven's provision to meet Earth's needs. If you are the facilitator of resourced provision then you need to identify signs that reveal whether or not you are effectively doing your job!

There are two questions you have to ask yourself when it comes to assessing your effectiveness as a facilitator of resources. The first question is "are you able to facilitate?" The second question is "are you actually facilitating?" To align with the message of this book, let's put these questions another way: "*can you pour?*" and "*are you pouring?*"

Truthfully answering the question "can you pour?" reveals your ability, as a vessel, to be continually refilled and emptied of divine resources in the completion of your purpose. It's a question that helps to assess your *wellness* in all its facets (i.e., spiritual, mental, emotional, and physical). Are you a poor vessel that is cracked, chipped, and corroded – leaking out what's been placed in you; or are you a vessel that can pour – one that is whole and able to hold and dispense the contents you were created to carry? If you are seeking to fulfill self then your wellness will likely become an afterthought because you don't need to be well or whole to receive. You can be spiritually broken and still make money; you can be emotionally fractured and still get bookings, offers, and opportunities afforded to you. However, if you are seeking to fulfill purpose then maintaining your wellness will remain a priority in your life because neither broken pitchers nor people can adequately pour. This is why the state of your wellness serves as a key indicator of your motives toward fulfilling self or purpose.

In addition to your wellness, the other key indicator of your motivation for fulfillment is your *expectation*; specifically, regarding what is produced from your allocated resources. Asking yourself the question "are you pouring?" is intended to get to the heart of your expectations for the effects of your outputs! It uncovers whether you are operating from a <u>poor</u> mindset that needs to profit or a <u>pour</u> mindset that needs to produce. When a pitcher/carafe pours coffee into a mug, it doesn't expect to get anything in return – not from the mug, not from the sugar dish, cream cup, or any other object – the only thing the carafe expects is to fill up the mug so the mug can be put to use in the fulfillment of its purpose. Likewise, when we have purpose-completing motives, we only expect what we pour out to fill gaps and meet needs, not to provide a personal profit. If you have an expectation of profit from the allocation of your resources, then you are making an investment for personal fulfillment, but if you have an expectation of your resources meeting needs, then you are making an impact for purpose-fulfillment – you are effectively pouring!

Wellness *(Can You Pour?)*
   Inclination: I identified wellness as a key indicator of

motives because of how society and conventional wisdom have continued to degrade its worth across generations. We humans have long viewed personal wellness as the necessary sacrifice for success, resulting in us placing our desires above and before our health and wellbeing. Particularly in America, we have embraced a cultural mindset that believes we aren't truly progressing towards success until we have begun to exhaust and ignore the vital elements our bodies require to thrive and flourish. Essential things such as sleep, food, relaxation, deep relational connections, and so forth have become bargaining chips for our self-fulfillment. But the truth is, when we are truly motivated to fulfill purpose, we strive to establish and maintain a healthy balance of these life essentials because damaged vessels can't adequately pour; meaning **your work can only impact at the level of your wellness**. This balance of wellness and work can only be accomplished when your work transcends the limitations of self-fulfillment and becomes an intentional and calculated self-emptying effort in the fulfillment of your purpose.

In terms of operating as an indicator for our motives, we know that we have started to move from purpose-fulfillment back to self-fulfillment when we start to consistently subject ourselves to "the grind". You are likely familiar with the term "on the grind" or "grinding", which speaks to the amount or difficulty of the work you are executing on a daily basis. The connotation is socially used to emphasize the ambitious pursuit that one is making to get what they want out of life – whether it be money, clout, recognition, etc. The grind is often viewed as an admirable attribute to have. However, if we look at the phrase from a different angle, we can see that, to a greater degree, it alludes to the grinding down of the person who is working to get all the things that they want. In that vein, when the perceived value of what you are striving for becomes greater than the value of your well-being, then you will resort to grinding away at your wellness to try and get it.

Complication: Subjecting ourselves to constant "grind" is a sign that we are responding to self-fulfilling motives to profit from what we provide, rather than purpose-fulfilling motives to make an impact through what we pour. Personal fulfillment is not concerned with wellness, only want. Therefore, your well-being is treated as an acceptable and sometimes even necessary causality in the process of attaining what you desire. Being motivated in this fashion is not only damaging, it is counter-intuitive because personal fulfillment will cause you to place healthy and holistic living on the altar of success by sacrificing the very thing (self) it is trying to fulfill.

This problematic thinking has become so glorified in our culture that people feel bad when they aren't losing sleep, skipping meals, foregoing vacations and time off, and avoiding meaningful relationships. God not only gave you a purpose, He also gave you the necessary being, or equipment (i.e. mind, body, and spirit) to fulfill it. Therefore, you cannot meet the intended objectives of your purpose without maintaining the equipment that's required to do it! When your wellness becomes depleted by the things you allow to drain you (i.e., jobs, dreams, toxic relationships, etc.) then you become limited in your ability to adequately seek, discern, and fulfill your God-given purpose.

Solution: If you are going to avoid "the grind", in order to complete your purpose, you have to keep wellness, not fullness, as your priority. You do so by striving to become a well-balanced, well-nourished, well-functioning person. A person who is capable of pouring into your purpose! Authentic fullness is not having all of your desires met, but because you were born full, it's the ability to effectively maintain what has already been placed within you; authentic fullness is not in competition with wellness, it is the result of wellness.

You will only aspire to prioritize wellness when you understand and believe that you have to be well in order to fulfill your purpose. Notice I said "well" and not "healthy" because some people have been subjected to health challenges that are out of their control, yet they are still very capable of pouring into their God-given purpose. Healthy is when your vital signs are at medically accepted levels, but being well is when you are functioning at your optimal status. In fact, I would venture to say that the illness or disability, of those who may not be medically "healthy", has ignited within them a commitment to wellness that informs and is very much aligned to the *Whats* of their purpose! It is impossible to pour from a depleted vessel, and therefore, your purpose can't be completed if your mind, body, and spirit are being drained.

You have to grow from being *drained* to being *emptied*. Being drained is when your vital resources are being used for a purpose that is not yours. Being emptied, on the other hand, only happens when you pour out your resources to fulfill your purpose. Emptying yourself to fulfill your purpose is a controlled and directed allocation of your resources. On the contrary, when you are being drained, you are unable to exercise portion control; the quality of your being and the quantity of your contents are not considered when being used. Emptying puts your wellness before your work. As such, it empowers you to strategically slow down your pour, if necessary, so you can be revitalized and refilled. However, when you are being drained, you allow your desire(s) to dictate when, how much, or for what use your resources, and ultimately your wellness, will be depleted. God is not in the business of refilling you for a purpose that He didn't give you, that's why you have to move from being drained to intentionally emptying yourself solely for your purpose by caring for your vessel.

Application: Progressing from being drained to being emptied requires you to assess and maintain the wholeness, or wellness, of your vessel in the context of your purpose. If it doesn't directly or indirectly align to, help complete, or support you in completing your purpose, then it lacks significance in your life and it's likely draining you of the resources your purpose requires. To identify and ultimately remove the "drainers" from your life, make a list with two separate columns next to each other. In the first column, list of all the things/people you are currently giving your God-given resources to (e.g. your time, money, gifts, talents, energy/effort, attention, etc.). In the second column, list all of the things/people currently aligned to your purpose. If you've completed the previous exercises then you should have a decent understanding of who they are. Finally, draw a line from the items in the first column to its match in the second column. If the thing/person in the first column doesn't have a match in the second column, then put a line through it.

Side Note: If you are not being paid to fulfill your

purpose and have another source of income (e.g., job, business, etc.) that you intentionally use to sustain yourself so you can fulfill your purpose for free, that source of income is still aligned to your purpose because it's financing its fulfillment! However, if the only reason you have that job or business is to get you all the things you want in life, if it's not freeing you to pour, then it's likely a drainer.

Once you've gone through the entire list, then assume that all the items with lines through them are drainers. Spend some time assessing why that thing/person has been afforded the privilege of consistently getting your resources when they are not aligned to your purpose. After reassessing that thing/person, if you determine that they are actually aligned to your purpose, add them back to the list. However, if you confirm that you are allowing them to drain you of what God has given you – to complete a purpose that is not yours – then strongly consider cutting them off!

By cutting off drainers, you should have more time, money, and energy, and so forth to allocate to your well-being. Be intentional about giving your mind/soul, body, and spirit what it needs to operate at its peak; exercise more, eat regularly and healthy, get adequate sleep, maintain deep connections with God and others, keep learning new things, and have fun! The goal is to start assessing your outputs from a perspective of wellness rather than fullness. It's likely that the things you were allowing to drain you made your life feel full (i.e., more friends, connections, activities, being wanted, etc.), but not well. God has given you everything you need to fulfill your purpose, not yourself! Purpose will never require you to be depleted in order for it to be completed; it needs your wellness, not your weakness.

Expectation *(Are You Pouring?)*

Inclination: We humans have a natural tendency to only allocate our resources to the people and situations that we believe will profit us in some form or fashion. A profit is the perceived value that something provides in excess of the value that was required to produce it. This type of investment approach to resource allocation often motivates the actions of those who are seeking self-fulfillment and are functioning outside of purpose. To be clear, there is nothing wrong with making invest-ments – allocating resources for a profit – but investing is not pouring and, therefore, it cannot fulfill your purpose!

The only type of resource allocation, which happens through authentic pouring and will enable you to fulfill your purpose, is sowing. Sowing is an agricultural term that defines the action of planting seeds in the ground in hope, or expectation, of producing a harvest. Both sowing and investing are able to produce a type of return, but the expectation of the sower and the investor differ. The investor expects to materialize **gain from** their resource, whereas the sower expects to materialize **growth through** their resource. Since personal gain is the investor's objective, they will only allocate their resources to self-serving things that they believe will provide them with what they want or feel they need. Investors expect something to come back to them; if there is no personal return provided, then the effort given to create the return seemingly has little to no value to the investor.

The sower, on the other hand, has an objective of growth that will motivate them to allocate their resources to things that will get the most out and make the most use of the resources (i.e. the seed) they sow. Sowers don't serve themselves, they serve the land (i.e. the people) they sow into because they know that the land is what yields the return. It will get the absolute most out of the seed they plant. The land doesn't just give the sower back more seed, it extracts what was dormant in the seed to produce something new; it has the ability to turn seeds into trees, shrubs, flowers, or fruit. Likewise, when it comes to purpose, sowers serve the people they allocate their resources to, only expecting that the people get the absolute most out of the resources they pour into them. This is why your expectations are a key indicator of your motives because those who are truly motivated to fulfill purpose are expecting the production of a sower, not the profit of an investor!

Complication: Having an investor's expectation of profit from the allocation of your God-given resources can be personally motivating and even personally lucrative. However, it is damaging to the completion of your purpose. Not only is this type of expectation an indicator that you have shifted from purpose-fulfillment to personal fulfillment, but when expected profit becomes the determining factor for when and where to allocate your resources, then you as the resource facilitator, become disconnected from the resource provider. In other words, you stop being directed by the intentions of God (i.e., God's purpose for your life) and start to be swayed and persuaded by your personal desires for gain. You stop expecting your resources to produce an impact in the world and start expecting them to provide a return back to you.

Beyond the inability to complete purpose, having a divine disconnect is what causes so many of us to experience emptiness (not to be confused with emptying ourselves to fulfill our purpose), lack of fulfillment, and incompleteness in our lives, even if we are receiving a personal profit from our invested resources. It's because **disconnection breeds isolation!** When you allow your self-influenced and self-fulfilling motives to disengage you from the intentions and direction of God, and from the needs of the people you were created to serve, then you subject yourself to the perils of isolation. You stop looking to be filled by your heavenly Supplier and attempt to be filled by the profit of your invested supply; you stop looking to pour into the people and places you've been assigned to and start trying to invest in what's profitable and culturally popular. Yes, you may experience a "come up" from your investments, but you will also experience being left out. You will be left out of the life-defining work that you were created to complete, left out of the flow of life-giving energy that comes from being in purposeful connection with your Higher Power and your peers, and be left out of the promises that God has given you; promises to strengthen and direct you in order to fulfill your purpose! Your profit can only provide you with more resources (e.g. time, money, connections, etc.) to manage, but it cannot satisfy nor complete you because nothing that comes from your hands can fill you! **The most necessary thing in and for your life – for your fulfillment and the fulfillment of your purpose – is not generating a personal**

profit, it's maintaining a life-enhancing connection with your Creator!

Solution: If you want to stay on the path to purpose-fulfillment you have to preserve and progress your relationship with God, who is your Creator, Supplier, and your Source. You have to cultivate the type of connection that relies solely on God to provide everything (i.e. resources and direction) you need to pour into and ultimately fulfill your purpose. Like a sower, you have to structure your expectations around productivity; expecting that the people you allocate your resources to will make the very best use of them. They will use your ideas to strategize and plan; they will use your money to build and develop; they will use your creativity, your expertise, your vision, etc. to do something that your resources, or theirs, couldn't accomplish on their own. You have to expect that they will turn your seeds into plants by taking what you pour out to them to produce the predestined impact you were born to make!

Having a sower's expectation is the result of one who sees the world, and their life, through the lens of their Creator. One who has adopted a "big picture" perspective and sees themselves as a necessary piece in a really big puzzle! Those who have an "individualistic" perspective see the world in themselves. They are aware of all that their environment has to offer them and they seek to obtain it. But those who have a "big picture" perspective see themselves in the world; they see all they have to offer to the world and its need for everything they have to offer. Yet, the only way to attain that viewpoint, to be able to operate from a "big picture" perspective, is to remain relationally connected to the One who is seated on high and only sees from that vantage.

Being in a relationship with my wife requires me to spend quality time with her and regularly converse with her in order to maintain and grow it. And it's in the cultivating of our relationship that I start to develop the ability to see things from her vantage point. I can look at a situation and already know how my wife will likely respond to it and how she will likely want me to respond to it because our connection helps me to interpret things from her perspective! Likewise, when I am in relationship with God – when I spend time talking to Him and listening to Him – I am able to see my surroundings and myself from His perspective. I am able to execute what He wants, how He wants, and have the right expectations for my efforts. To have an expectation that considers my resources to be seed and not feed, understanding that God fulfills me and I, in turn, fulfill my purpose!

Application: You now know that the solution to maintaining a sower's expectation while allocating your resources is to remain connected to God. What may not be so clear, are the practical steps you should take to do that. Laying out a clear-cut path to initiating, developing, and maintaining a fruitful relationship with the Creator and Ruler of the universe is a difficult, if not impossible, task to say the least. Each person reading this book has different spiritual foundations, different experiences and world views that shape their image of God, as well as different communication and relational predispositions. Therefore, to attempt to whittle down the totality of a divine relationship into a few steps would require me to grossly over-generalize and over-assume, which I believe would be both irresponsible and un-impactful.

Taking all of that into consideration, there may not only be one type of relationship that a human being can have with God, however, despite the specific channels and complexities of your personal relationship, there are some key elements that every divine relationship should have. For example, when I say communication is a key element, I am not saying that we all need to communicate with God the same way; I'm simply saying that we should all be communicating with God in some way, medium, or form. The reason you must instill these key connection elements into your relationship with the Divine is because each element, if implemented properly, will help to shape you into the person you were created to be; one who is actively pouring to fulfill their God-given purpose in all its many facets.

These elements will help to shape both your **heart** and **mind** to align with your Creator's intention for your life so that you can pour how God wants you to pour and expect from it what God wants you to expect. Your heart and mind are the most vital parts of how you function because your heart is your place of *distribution* (Luke 6:45) and your mind is your place of *discernment* (Romans 12:2). They work in tandem to regulate what you put out into the world and what you take in from it, respectively.

> **Luke 6:45b** - *"...for it is out of the abundance of the heart that the mouth speaks."* [1]

> *You will only distribute to the world that which is resident in your heart; therefore, your heart will determine what you pour. It is the dwelling place of your desires; within it lies your will, your way, and your intentions. The substance of your heart*

dictates what you value, what you pursue, what you say and do to/for people, what you produce and create, and so forth.

If you stop pouring into purpose, it's not because your heart is empty of the right things but rather because it's full of the wrong things! A heart full of self will cause you to restrict, or even restrain, your resources to attain or maintain personal-fulfillment; you will only distribute what you believe will profit you. Conversely, a heart full of service will make you distribute your resources for purpose-fulfillment; you will pour into gaps to meet needs, produce change, and cultivate growth around you. You cannot separate the content of your character from the contents of your heart, because the only thing that can pour out of you is what abides within you.

Romans 12:2a - *"Do not be conformed to this world, but be transformed by the renewing of your minds, so that you may discern what is the will of God..."* [2]

What you grasp and discern from what you experience in your life is determined by the frame of your mind! Just like a portrait frame encases a painting, your mind encases your experiences and will only allow you to see and assess what fits within it. If you have a limited frame, then you have a limited view and, in turn, will have a limited understanding of what is happening to and around you. Therefore, to gain a better understanding of your role on and in the earth, you have to renew, or reframe, your mind to see the world as God sees it; you have to broaden the borders of your mind to see the big picture and maintain a purpose-filling outlook on life.

An un-renewed mind can see the same thing as a renewed mind and yet will draw a different conclusion, not only because it is limited in perspective (what it sees) but also because of its limited perception (what it interpret from what it sees)! In other words, inspecting your surroundings through the lens of a renewed mind not only helps you to see what God wants you to see, but it enables you to reason, or discern, how God wants you to reason. He wants you to see the picture from His perspective of everyone's needs, not just your own; He also wants you to discern what you see, considering His abundance, not your lack!

An un-renewed mind of Lack will look at an area of responsibility (e.g., employment, marriage, parenthood, client requests, volunteer assignments, etc.) and only see what it has to offer you. It provides a limited perspective that only lends itself to reasoning which expects an investor's return for your distributed resources. It sees what your boss, your spouse, and your children aren't doing and says "because I've given to them, I deserve and need more from them, in order to be fulfilled."

On the other hand, a renewed mind of Abundance will look at the same areas and not focus on what they have to offer you, but see their need and the resources you possess to alleviate it. It will afford you a "big picture" perspective that promotes divine discernment to convict and support an intentional response of pouring. It sees the needs of your boss, spouse, and kids that you are equipped to address and says, "because my resources are not finite, my purpose is not personal, and I was made to remedy – not to exploit – these needs, I will pour into them." Divine discernment only expects a sower's return of growth in your areas of responsibility, from the purposeful allocation of your resources!

The nature of your relationship with God, or the lack thereof, will shape the contents of your heart which produces your pour, and the frame of your mind which informs your expectations. If you want a relationship that preserves a heart and mind-shaping connection with God, then you need to make sure that it encompasses these three key elements:

1.) Communication: This is nothing more than having an open exchange with God, where you share yourself (i.e. your thoughts, fears, hopes, needs, and so on) with Him, and in turn, you seek His will (i.e. His guidance, understanding, and plans) for you. As I mentioned before, there are numerous ways to communicate with God and, honestly, I would recommend incorporating many, if not all, of them into an ongoing routine because you never know how you will best connect with him, at various points in your life. You can exchange with God in prayer by speaking to Him; in meditation by quieting your voice and listening for His; in reading scripture, which will help you understand what God is saying by seeing what He has already said and done! Each of these forms of exchange will enable you to not only encounter God in different ways, but will help to shape your heart and mind to discern, desire, pursue, and pour what He wants for and from you.

2.) Trust: Having an undying trust in the presence and promises of God is key to maintaining a strong connection with Him. It's necessary because there will be times in your life when you will question and doubt the validity of both. When you encounter trying times and difficult situations, it will feel as if God is not with you and that all the things He has communicated to you, in meditation and scripture, weren't true and won't happen. Like in any meaningful relationship, the value of trust is not revealed until doubt and unbelief are present, and so it is in your relationship with the Divine! When you have trust in God, you will be able to sustain a sower's expectation; you will be able to confidently pour your resources out to those in need, trusting that God will be with you through it all and keep his promise to refill you when you think you have nothing left to give.

Not only is trust needed to overcome moments of doubt in a relationship, but it is necessary to create dependence. Trust is a two-way street; it is required for you to depend on God, but also for Him to depend on you! When it comes to implementing trust in your divine relationship, you can't just look to God to see if He is holding up His end of the bargain, you have to also look in the mirror to assess if you are holding up yours. Are you being faithful in the work He has assigned you to, are you following His direction, are you relying on your investments to provide for you or are you pouring into your purpose believing He is your source? Can God trust you with the resources and the requirement He has given you, or not?

The beauty of real trust is that it can't be bought or borrowed, it can only be built! You build trust with God by learning to lean and rely on Him rather than on yourself! There are a number of practices you can institute to become less dependent on your human proclivities and instinct (i.e. self), and more dependent on the spiritual, but one effective way is to fast. When you give up something that appeals to the desires of your physical self in exchange for time and attention given to God, then you will start to see that what's comforting you is not what's keeping you! You will uncover that your best life – your peak performance, your highest quality, your greatest efficiency, and your optimal capacity – can only be realized by trusting your Manufacturer and following His instructions, so you can effectively function as He designed.

3.) Commitment: In terms of characterizing a relationship, the word "commitment" expresses two major aspects of what that relationship should consist of. The first aspect is *dedication*! Both parties engaged in a thriving, reciprocating relationship need to be dedicated to its development; I say "development" because many people, after years of being together, stop being dedicated to the development of the relationship and simply dedicate themselves to its survival. In terms of being in a relationship with God, this looks like exercising religious practices absent of authentic communication and trust; there's acknowledgement of His presence but no intimacy or interaction with Him. Dedication is what you consciously and consistently put into a relationship; your dedication to God is manifested through your daily devotion of time, attention, and effort to Him, His word, and His will. God has dedicated Himself to you as well. He never leaves you nor forsakes you, He orders the steps in front of you, and assigns Goodness and Mercy to follow you every day. He is devoted to your well-being and to your divine destination!

The second major aspect of commitment is *obligation*. Dedication is what you give to a relationship to make it thrive, but obligation is what you give up to remain in a thriving relationship. A great relationship is like a beautiful rose bush, it not only requires you to put water and sunlight into it, it requires you to prune debilitating things off of it. There is a tax that is excised on a divine relationship because attaining a heart and mind-shaping connection with God has a cost. It will cost you your pride, your ego, your will, and your way. Like the rose bush, the only way you will grow, to see how He sees and discern how He discerns, is to die to yourself and allow him to prune the debilitating parts of who you are by submitting yourself to Him.

The good news is that you are not alone in your death; just like you sacrifice yourself to enhance your connection with God, He also sacrificed Himself to establish and enhance His connection with you! He sent his only begotten son, who died on a cross to obligate Himself to your relationship and there is no greater love than to lay down your life for those you are in a relationship with. The better news is that, just like Christ's death was not final, neither is yours! There is life on the other side of your self-sacrifice, a life that God and the world both have great need of and is destined to make an indelible impact in every person and place you pour into!

Chapter 7

PERMISSION TO POUR

The title of this chapter is not meant to imply that you, as an adult, need permission to pour out your God-given resources to others; neither is it intended to insinuate that even if you did need permission, I am the one to grant it. No, the wording is not to authorize you to pour, but rather to empower and encourage you to do so! Permitting you to pour is essentially my way of putting the ball in your court, to start executing on the requirements of your purpose. It's an excuse remover for all of you who feel like you have to have it all together, all figured out, and all in place before you can start making a purpose-driven impact. When it comes to pouring, the best time to do it is in the time that you have, which is not in the past nor the future, but right now!

I have recruited, organized, and deployed every word of this book to defeat any excuse that might attempt to delay or hinder you from pouring to fulfill your purpose. Some of you haven't poured into your purpose because you're waiting to find out what your purpose is; a number of you haven't poured because you're waiting to first be fulfilled; others of you haven't poured because you're waiting to be validated and affirmed by people. Whatever your excuse has been up until this very point, it's no longer relevant because, regardless of its magnitude, it's not bigger than your purpose. The world can do without another excuse, but it cannot do without your resources, your service, and your giving; those connected to your purpose don't need you to be perfect, they just need you to pour!

For those of you who are still succumbed to doubt and obscurity about what to do, you who are remaining stagnant because you're uncertain about what actions to take and what people to connect to, allow me to give you a little push. When it comes to pouring into your purpose, the best way to discover what actions you should be taking and what people you should be connecting with, is to start taking action and start connecting with people! Many purpose-seeking people remain at a standstill – only analyzing their purpose, but not fulfilling it – because they've made their service dependent on certainty. They withstand serving the needs of others until they are certain that their efforts will produce the impact they desire; certain their time, energy, and money won't be wasted; certain that their work won't be taken for granted and so on. However, the only thing that is guaranteed to come from your service is experience, which I've learned is far more valuable than many of the things you are currently looking for your pour to produce in and through your life.

Experience will start to operate as your eyes and ears when discerning what initiatives to execute, who to do them for, and who to do them with. The experience of starting a contracting firm helped me to discover that it wasn't a part of my purpose; the experience of having a child revealed that I can't fulfill my purpose apart from being the best dad I can be; my experience writing this book, in light of all its many challenges and schedule delays, clarified that this was an unavoidable avenue (i.e. one of my *Whats*) that I had to pour through! It's not analysis and advice that perfects your pour, it's the wisdom gained from your experiences pouring whenever, however, and wherever you can that enables you to streamline your flow of resources over time to fulfill your purpose.

With every pour experience – every attempt to alleviate a persistent need of another – revelation is manifested. Pouring reveals your internal deficiencies (pursuing the wrong things) and your external drainers (the wrong things pulling from you), which is the valuable information you need to make the necessary adjustments to your flow. Fulfilling purpose through pouring is an exercise of adjustment. Similar to handling the steering wheel while driving a car, perfecting your pour is about constant correction. You can't hold the steering wheel in the same position if you want to stay inside your designated lane while driving; you have to keep adjusting it due to the changing road conditions. Likewise, you have to constantly make small adjustments to your pour, based on the information your experiences present to you, while you are serving others through your giving.

The more that's revealed to you, the more you will need to adjust to better focus your flow on fulfilling purpose! Perhaps you will need to disconnect from certain people that you weren't intended to pour into. You may even need to choose a different avenue or outlet to pour from or adjust to changing needs by providing a different resource that you possess. Maybe your personal circumstances and needs will start to contaminate your efforts and you will have to make corrections to get back to filtering your flow through service rather than self. Regardless of the adjustments that you need to make along your journey to completing your purpose, the one thing you must continue to do, at whatever capacity your wellness requires, is to pour – serving the needs of others through your giving, only expecting your efforts to produce growth that positively impacts the people you are connected to.

Let me say that one more time, "Don't stop pouring!" The hardest thing to do, outside of starting to pour, is to keep pouring. This sentiment is not exclusive to fulfilling purpose, it's a reality in every area of our lives that require discipline. It's hard to start working out, it's even harder to keep working out. It's hard to start eating healthy, but it's way more difficult to stick with it. It's difficult to start a business, but managing one and making it profitable is another beast in and of itself. Acknowledging this fact is important to reaching the ultimate goal of fulfilling your purpose because, without it, I would be setting you up for failure. As sugar-coated as I would like it to be, the truth is, you will be faced with many trying situations and circumstances that, if not anticipated and responded to efficaciously, will cause you to stop pouring and abandon your purpose!

Remember that your pour is predicated on your need to release what has been placed within you, the abundance of resources at your disposal, and the needs of those you were created to connect to. This means that despite your survival instincts, your inner circle, and even societal norms trying to convince you otherwise, your ability to pour is not dependent on your shortcomings. It's not dependent on your finances, your heart break, your losses, your sickness, your disappointments, or your bad decisions, etc. No matter what you end up going through, as long as you're living, you still possess heaven's provision for a world that is still in dire need of it. Therefore, you still have the responsibility and the capability to pour.

This may sound a bit dismissive and insensitive because it initially comes off as if I am saying "get over whatever you're dealing with so you can keep pouring." However, that's not the case. I'm actually suggesting the opposite, I'm saying "keep pouring so you can get over/through whatever you're dealing with!" When life hits you the hardest, you will feel as if you have nothing left to give, or at the very best, nothing worth giving. You will tell yourself hidden lies that appear to be truthful on the surface, things like "I'm too broke to give", "I'm too hurt to give", "I'm too sick to give", etc. Yet, having endured financial struggles, rejection, loss, and pain for myself, I can say from experience that the best way to combat the lies of not having anything to give, is to start giving.

Pouring when you think you're tapped out not only disproves the negative self-talk that we all subject ourselves to in tough times, but it's also a morale booster! Pouring through pain may not remove the pain you're subjected to, but it will change how you view it, respond to it, and move through it. Pouring will cause you to dig deep within yourself to access resources you didn't know you had; to cross paths with people in places that you would have otherwise never met or visited; to deepen and develop your life-giving/healing/enhancing relationship with your Creator. I'm not suggesting you ignore your pain, I'm encouraging you to heal where you hurt while you pour from where you're healthy. If finances are low, perhaps give your time. If time is low, then give your talent, but whatever you do, don't stop serving others. Serving through your suffering will provide you with purpose-defining experiences that will enable you to perfect your pour!

No matter where you are in life, no matter what you've been through, or what you've yet to accomplish, now is your time! It's your time to fulfill your purpose, it's your time to become the person you were created to be, it's your time to make a needed and undeniable impact right where you are. It's your time to pour, so go ahead – you have my permission!

NOTES

1. A Greater End

1. Gen. 1:26-27 NRSV (The Zondervan Corporation, L.L.C., 2010)
2. Gen. 2:4b-6 NRSV (The Zondervan Corporation, L.L.C., 2010)

2. More Than Work

1. (Merriam-Webster, Incorporated, 2019)

3. Filter Your Flow

1. Matt. 20:28a NRSV (The Zondervan Corporation, L.L.C., 2010)

4. From Self to Service

1. Simply Psychology: Maslow's Hierarchy of Needs (McLeod, 2018)

6. From Poor to Pour

1. Luke 6:45b NRSV (The Zondervan Corporation, L.L.C., 2010)
2. Rom. 12:2a NRSV (Zondervan Corporation, L.L.C, 2010)

ACKNOWLEDGMENTS

When I think of extending thanks, the first person that comes to mind is my amazing wife Tiffany, who not only contributed with her written words, but with her spoken prayers and words of encouragement. Our in-depth conversations about purpose and motives pulled acumen and understanding out of me that I didn't know was present! For that and countless other acts of sacrifice and support, I thank and love you! I have to thank my daughter, Ava, who has unintentionally placed a responsibility of legacy on my shoulders that I hope this book helps to carry. It's my desire that these words will one day help her and her sibling(s) fulfill their God-given purpose and ultimately change the world for the better.

I must thank all four of my parents! To my mom (Cheryl) and dad (Greg), I am forever grateful for the foundation of love and commitment that you both set for my brothers (Marcus & Trent) and myself. Your refusal to give up and insistence to give thanks through good and bad times has imparted to me a healthy mix of tenacity and humility that enables me to serve God and others in all my endeavors. To my mother-in-law/ "Ma" (Kellie), thank you for always being exited for the seemingly small things in our lives and encouraging me to give credence to the meaningful life occurrences that my ambition would otherwise cause me to overlook or take for granted. To my father-in-law/ "Pops" (Leonard), I am thankful for your consistent example and your steady counsel; your commitment to helping to develop me as a person, and not just my gifts, is something that I don't always enjoy but, evidenced by the fruit it produces, is something I do need and appreciate! I give thanks to and for my brothers, who let me practice being a parent before I ever had kids. My goal, as your big brother, was to impart knowledge to you, but in turn, I've learned much more than I've taught – which I am truly grateful for.

It is absolutely necessary that I acknowledge the Daquins and the Dickersons who have been in the foxhole with us throughout this entire journey. From praying and fasting with me to giving me valuable feedback, even texting celebratory "GIFs" for every small win along the way, your support has been unwavering and I'm gratefully indebted to each of you! To *The Crew*, you all are a rare breed! The word "friendship" is inadequate to capture what we've developed, our bond is more like soil that nourishes all who are planted in it – I want to thank each of you for the laughs, advice, and inspiration that has fed my growth over the years! I want to acknowledge my grandparents, – those with me in person and spirit – my extended family of loved ones (aunts, uncles, and cousins), and my church family all of whom have had a hand in my personal development.

Last but not least, I want to thank myself; I want to thank *me* for pushing through the doubt, writer's block, lack of conviction, schedule constraints, competing priorities, procrastination, ignorance, inexperience, previous failures, missed opportunities, and lack of focus. Congrats Merrick on finding your voice amid all the noise!

Made in the USA
Middletown, DE
11 January 2020

83018033R10082